Intermediate

Student's Book

Jayne Wildman David Bolton

OXFORD
UNIVERSITY PRESS

Contents

		READING	GRAMMAR	VOCABULARY
1	**Away from home** page 4	- Different countries, different customs - Far from home	- Present simple and present continuous - Stative verbs - The gerund - *want*	- Compound nouns - Adverbs of degree
2	**A job for life?** page 12	- Students at work - High-flyer	- Past simple and past continuous - Past perfect - *used to* - *get used to / be used to*	- Adjectives of character - The world of work
Units 1–2 revision		pages 20–21	Revision of main language points	
3	**Teenage blues** page 22	- The best years? - The last laugh	- Comparatives and superlatives - Other comparative forms - Quantifiers	- Education: verb + noun - Phrasal verbs: friendship
4	**Taking risks** page 30	- No limits - Life on a high wire	- Present perfect simple - *for* and *since* - *already*, *just* and *yet* - Present perfect and past simple	- Phrasal verbs: *look* - Adventure sports - Prepositions of movement
Units 3–4 revision		pages 38–39	Revision of main language points	
5	**Natural disasters** page 40	- Hotshot firefighters - Cumbre Vieja	- *will*, *going to* and the present continuous - Future continuous - Future perfect	- Word building - Weather
6	**Fears and phobias** page 48	- What are you scared of? - What's in a number?	- Passive: present and past - Passive: present perfect - *have / get something done*	- Confusing words - Adjective + preposition
Units 5–6 revision		pages 56–57	Revision of main language points	
7	**Inventions** page 58	- A dream come true - Inventions that changed the world	- First and second conditional - *unless* - Third conditional	- *make* and *do* - Idioms - Synonyms
8	**First impressions** page 66	- Street life - The Doc Marten Story	- Defining relative clauses - Non-defining relative clauses	- Describing appearance - Phrasal verbs: *take*
Units 7–8 revision		pages 74–75	Revision of main language points	
9	**Travellers' tales** page 76	- The long road west - Any excuse	- Reported speech: statements - Time expressions in reported speech - Reported speech: questions and commands - Reported speech: suggestions	- Phrasal verbs: *travel* - Phrasal verbs: *get* - Adverbs of manner
10	**Fame** page 84	- Public property - Drummer who said 'no' to the stones	- Modals: ability - Modals: obligation, advice and prohibition - Modals: possibility and certainty - Modals + perfect infinitive	- Money - Talking about prices - Phrasal verbs: the music industry
Units 9–10 revision		pages 92–93	Revision of main language points	

Songbook pages 94–98   **Grammar reference** pages 99–110   **Irregular verb list** page 111

LISTENING	SPEAKING AND PRONUNCIATION	WRITING	WORKBOOK EXTENSION
Checking information about first impressions	Discussing first impressions of your country	Informal letters Writing a letter to a friend	Verb + infinitive or –ing Opposites: verbs
Completing job interview forms	Conducting a job interview	Brainstorming ideas Explaining job choices	would for past habits Verb + noun: jobs and work
Identifying details in descriptions of friends	Discussing the qualities a friend should have	Linking words: time sequencers Describing an extraordinary event	neither (of) and both (of) Adverbs of manner
Checking information about extreme sport	Sentence stress Discussing dangerous or frightening experiences	Linking words: contrast, reason and result Describing a dangerous or frightening event	still and yet been and gone More linking words
Identifying key information in a weather report	Giving a news report about a natural disaster	Relevant information Explaining the causes and effects of extreme weather	Time expressions Geographical words
Completing details about a strange encounter	Weak forms: was and were Describing a strange dream	Paragraphing Writing a for and against essay	Future passive Abstract uncountable nouns
Identifying inventions from descriptions	Asking and answering questions about inventions	Planning Writing an article about a new invention	Conditionals with unless, as long as and in case Units of measurement
Identifying responses to a questionnaire	Words containing silent letters Completing a questionnaire about image	Formal letters Writing a letter of complaint	Defining relative clauses: omitting the pronoun Words to describe faults or problems
Identifying information about different travel options	Asking for and giving tourist information	Checking for accuracy Writing a story about a difficult or disastrous journey	Reporting verbs Compound nouns: travel
Checking information from an interview	Words containing the sound /ɔː/ Interviewing someone from a pop star academy	Checking content Setting out the arguments for and against being famous	need Adjectives: people and objects

1 Away from home

INTRODUCTION

1 Imagine you are living away from home, in a different country. Which three things in the box do you think you would miss the most? Which would you not miss? Give reasons for your answers.

> your friends   people who speak your language
> favourite TV programmes   your family   school
> a pet   news of what's happening in your country
> your favourite food   your boyfriend / girlfriend

READING

2 Look at the pictures and the title of the text on page 5. What do you think the text is about? Choose the best alternative.
 a A holiday in Britain.
 b Reasons for coming to Britain.
 c Living in Britain.

3 Read the text and check your answer.

4 Read the text again. Are the sentences true or false?
 1 It's easy for young people to get a job in Britain.
 2 English drivers are quite aggressive.
 3 People prefer to live in tall buildings in London.
 4 When Berna first came to England she apologized a lot.
 5 Cassio trains in the morning and the afternoon.
 6 The players go home after they've finished training.
 7 Cassio uses his computer in his hotel room.
 8 The fans don't like foreign players.

5 Find words and phrases in the text with similar meanings to:
 1 disadvantages (paragraph E)
 2 say sorry (paragraph F)
 3 practise (paragraph I)
 4 enjoy themselves (paragraph I)
 5 flat (paragraph I)
 6 unbelievably (paragraph K)

DISCUSSION

6 Discuss the questions.
 1 Why do some people live abroad?
 2 What are the advantages and disadvantages of living abroad?
 3 Do you think you'll ever live or work abroad? Why / Why not?
 4 Where would you like to go?
 5 Would you stay there for ever or would you come back to your own country? Why?

4   Unit 1

Different countries, different customs

A | Berna Kayhan is Turkish. She's studying engineering at London University.

G | Cassio Oliveira is a professional footballer from Brazil. He plays for a Scottish club.

'They just sit and wait. Amazing!'

B | Everything's very different here. For a start, money's not a problem for young people. When they've got some they spend it, without worrying about the future. When they haven't got any left they get a job and earn some more.

C | What else? I love the way English drivers are so patient. If there's a traffic jam, they don't sit with their hand on the horn or try to jump the queue. They just sit and wait. Amazing!

D | People seem to live much nearer the ground, even in London, rather than in tall blocks of flats. Houses in the city centre even have their own gardens.

E | But there are some downsides to living here. For example, there's so little light. It's like living in a room with only a single 40 watt bulb. And the people are very private, enclosed within themselves. They look after their own business and they're not really interested in other people's.

F | One more thing; when I first came to England, all I heard was 'I'm sorry', 'excuse me', 'please', and 'thank you'. The English are much too polite. They apologize even when they've done nothing wrong!

'It's so incredibly cold!'

H | 'In Brazil it's usually hot. But here in Scotland it's extremely cold and it rains or snows every day. I often want to wear a hat and gloves when I play, but I think the other players might laugh at me.

I | We train in the morning and then we go to a café together to talk and have a laugh. After that I go back to my hotel room and I spend a lot of time on my laptop. I surf the Internet and send emails to my family and to my girlfriend – Sheena. She's a student at Edinburgh University. She's studying psychology. The hotel's OK but I'm looking for my own apartment.

J | In the evening I usually go out. I often see the fans when I'm out. They're wonderful. They love their team but they also respect your privacy. People say "Hi", but they don't stop me and ask why we lost last Saturday.

K | I enjoy living in Scotland. It's just a pity it's so incredibly cold!'

GRAMMAR

PRESENT SIMPLE AND PRESENT CONTINUOUS

1 Match the sentences with the rules.
a Oh no! It**'s raining**.
b She**'s studying** engineering this year.
c We **train** in the morning.
d People **live** much nearer the ground.
e What time **are you meeting** Cassio tonight?

> We use the present simple to talk about:
> 1 habits or regular activities.
> 2 facts or things that are generally true.
>
> We use the present continuous to talk about:
> 3 things that are in progress now.
> 4 temporary situations.
> 5 future arrangements.

2 Complete the sentences. Use one verb twice in each sentence. Use the correct form of the present simple and the present continuous.

> ~~shine~~   go   live   have   enjoy   play   write   train

The sun *doesn't shine* a lot in Scotland but *it's shining* at the moment.

1 Berna _____ back to Turkey as often as possible, but it's February now and she _____ back till next summer.
2 She _____ to her parents today, but her British friends _____ to their parents because they see them every weekend.
3 For the moment she _____ in a flat with some friends, but in Turkey she _____ with her family.
4 It's 8 o'clock and Cassio _____ dinner. In Brazil he usually _____ dinner at 10 o'clock.
5 Cassio normally _____ with the football team, but today he _____ on his own.
6 He normally _____ training but it's cold today so he _____ it at all!
7 Cassio _____ football six days a week but this evening he _____ a computer game with his girlfriend, Sheena.

3 Complete the telephone conversation. Use the present simple and the present continuous.

Cassio   Hi Sheena, how are you?
Sheena   (1) I / be / fine, thanks. *I'm fine thanks.*
Cassio   (2) What / do / tonight?
Sheena   (3) First I / cook / dinner. Then I / finish / some work for my course.
Cassio   (4) You / like / your course?
Sheena   (5) Yes, but psychology / be / very difficult.
Cassio   (6) You / come / to the match on Saturday?
Sheena   (7) Yes. I / hope / to get a lift with a friend.
Cassio   (8) Your friend / enjoy / watching football?
Sheena   (9) Yes, but she / support / the other team!

4 Ask and answer questions in pairs.
Family
1 You / live / with your family?
Education
2 How many subjects / you / study / this year?
3 You / go / to university / after / leave / school?
Free time
4 How often / you / play / computer games?
5 You / surf / the Internet?
6 What / you / do / this evening?
Personality
7 You / worry / about the future?
8 How / patient and polite / you / think / you / be?

5 Prepare an extra question for each topic in Exercise 4. Ask and answer them in pairs.

STATIVE VERBS

6 Read the sentences and complete the rule. Use *present simple* or *present continuous*.
a I **like** computer games but I **hate** football.
b I don't **understand**.

> Some verbs are almost never used in the _____ tense.
> The most common stative verbs are:
> be   believe   forget   hate   know   like   love   mean   remember   see   understand   want

7 These sentences contain mistakes. Find and correct the mistakes.

I'm not liking foreign food.
I don't like foreign food.

1 'What type of music are you liking?' 'I love hip-hop.'
2 I'm not understanding what you're saying.
3 I'm forgetting Ann's surname. Do you remember it?
4 'What does this word mean?' 'I'm not remembering.'

Grammar reference page 99

VOCABULARY

COMPOUND NOUNS

1 Complete the compound nouns. Use the words in the box.

> washing   alarm   hair   CD   pen   laptop
> credit   tin   mobile   coffee

1 _____ clock
2 _____ maker
3 _____ machine
4 _____ phone
5 _____ player
6 _____ opener
7 _____ dryer
8 _____ knife
9 _____ computer
10 _____ card

2 What do you notice about the way these compound nouns are spelt? Are there any spelling rules for compound nouns? Note down the spelling of each new word.

> washing-machine   alarm clock   hairdryer

3 Complete the sentences. Use the compound nouns from Exercise 1.

1 I wash all my clothes by hand because they don't have a _____ here.
2 My flight leaves early but I don't need an _____ . I'll wake up anyway.
3 I can work on my _____ while I'm waiting at the airport.
4 If you want to speak to me while I'm away, try my _____ .
5 I brought my _____ with me because I need a hot drink first thing in the morning.
6 My hair looks a mess after I've washed it because I haven't brought a _____ with me.
7 I take my _____ with me when I go on picnics. It can cut things and open bottles.
8 I haven't got a TV in my room, but I often listen to music on my _____ .
9 You can't pay for anything by _____ . They only accept cash.
10 I cook for myself. The thing I use most in the kitchen is a _____ .

4 Imagine you're going to live away from home for a year. Discuss in groups how important the things in Exercise 1 will be to you. Put the things in order starting with the most important. Use the phrases to help you.

I (don't) think a ... is very important.
I must have a ...
I (don't) really need a ...
I couldn't live without ...

Unit 1   **7**

READING

1 Look at the pictures and the title of the text. What do you think the text is about?

2 Read the text and check your answer.

3 Read the text again and answer the questions.
1. Why do Tibetan parents send their sons to the monastery?
2. Why are the boys easy to teach?
3. How many days a week does Nick work?
4. Why is it important for the boys to remember the scriptures they learn?
5. What part do cockroaches play in Nick's life?
6. Why does Nick envy the boys he teaches?

4 Would you like to be a student or a teacher in a school like Nick's? Why / Why not?

5 Match the words from the text with the definitions.
1. desperate (line 12)
2. recite (line 20)
3. scriptures (line 21)
4. cockroaches (line 25)
5. candle (line 32)
6. regret (line 40)

a. the holy books of a religion
b. you burn this to give light
c. feel sorry
d. extremely keen
e. large, dark brown insects that are often found in hot countries
f. say aloud something that was written

6 Answer the questions about the phrases from the text.

... takes education for granted
1. What do you take for granted?
2. What do your parents take for granted?

... they're in serious trouble
3. When or why are you in serious trouble with your parents or your teachers?

... the consumer goods we have
4. Which of the following do you think are not consumer goods? Why?

> CD player   washing-machine   food
> mobile phone   laptop computer   education
> vacuum cleaner   electric light

Far from home

Nick Kennedy got a job in a Tibetan monastery after leaving school, before going to university. He's teaching English and science to huge classes of boys aged nine to eighteen.

5 In the West everybody takes education for granted. Tibetans don't. For Tibetan parents it's the most important gift they can give their children because it's their best, and perhaps only, chance in life. Above all, Tibetans want their sons to have an
10 education. The boys in the monastery want Nick to teach them everything he knows because they're desperate to learn.

They work extremely hard for six days a week which means that he only gets one
15 day off a week, too. The idea of having a whole free weekend amazes them. They get up at five and learn Tibetan scriptures for two hours. School finishes at five. They then have one hour free when they usually
20 play basketball. From six till eight they recite the scriptures they learnt in the morning. If they don't know them, they're in serious trouble with their teachers.

Nick sleeps in a very small room with just a bed and cockroaches for company. The cockroaches like hiding in his 25 clothes, so he has to be very careful when he gets dressed. 'I enjoy hunting them. To tell you the truth, hunting cockroaches is my only entertainment in the evening. I can't read because there's no electric light in my room, 30 only a small candle.'

He gets the same food as the boys – rice and vegetables for every meal. 'That's what I dream about most – chicken and 35 hamburgers.' He hasn't got a toothbrush so he cleans his teeth with a stick or the end of a pencil. The top student at the end of the year gets a toothbrush as a prize.

Nick doesn't regret coming to Tibet. 'I like 40 teaching and I envy the boys I teach. I really think they're happy. They don't know anything about the consumer goods we have, or want to have, so their lives are much simpler. I want to be like them but I've grown up in the 45 West so for me it's too late.'

Unit 1

GRAMMAR

THE GERUND

1 Read the sentences and match them to the uses.
  a The idea of **having** a free weekend amazes them.
  b **Hunting** cockroaches is my only entertainment.
  c The cockroaches like **hiding** in his clothes.

> We use the gerund:
> 1 as the subject of a sentence.
> 2 after certain verbs.
> 3 after prepositions.

2 Find eight examples of the gerund in the paragraph. Decide why the gerund is used in each example.

> Nick is living in Tibet for a year. He's enjoying it and he doesn't regret coming to Tibet. He's earning very little, but that is not a problem because he isn't interested in earning a lot of money. He enjoys teaching but teaching big classes is very difficult. Living in Tibet isn't easy, though. He eats the same food every day but he dreams of eating chicken and hamburgers. In the evening he enjoys hunting cockroaches. Nick isn't very good at writing letters but he writes home every week.

3 Eleni is a Greek student living in Ireland. Correct the mistakes in her sentences.

> I came to Ireland two months after ~~to leave~~ *leaving* school.

1 I thought about to go straight to university.
2 I enjoy live on my own and being independent.
3 But to improve my English was more important.
4 I like meeting people and I'm good at talk to them.
5 After to live with an aunt for a month, I got my own room.
6 To find a room was very difficult.

4 Complete the sentences. Use the gerund of the verbs in brackets and add information about you.

> Before (come) *coming* to school, I *have breakfast*.

1 After (leave) _____ school, I ... .
2 I like (live) _____ at home because ... .
3 I'm interested in (learn) _____ more about ... .
4 I enjoy (play) _____ with ... .

WANT

5 Look at the word order in these examples.

The boys **want** + **Nick** + **to teach** *them*
        1   2   3

Tibetans **want** + **their children** + **to have** *an education.*
         1   2   3

1 Are the words in box 2 the subject or the object of the sentence?
2 What form of the verb comes in box 3?

6 Put the words in the correct order.

1 want we to university you the tell about us
2 you I listen want to
3 come don't want I them to
4 work hard me to want my parents
5 you with I come want me to
6 students want teachers to their understand

7 Complete the sentences. Use *want* + object + infinitive.

> My parents / me / go / to / university
> *My parents want me to go to university.*

1 Most parents / their children / enjoy / school
2 Our teachers / us / work / hard
3 The students in our class / our teacher / help / us
4 I / my friend / live / near me
5 My father / me / become / a doctor
6 My younger brother / us / lend / him some money

Grammar reference page 99

Unit 1   9

VOCABULARY

ADVERBS OF DEGREE

1 Look at the pictures. Who's working hard and who's working extremely hard?

Tom   Joe

2 Complete the table. Use the adverbs of degree in the box.

| extremely a bit slightly really rather pretty totally fairly exceptionally absolutely completely |

Very (++)	_____
Quite (+)	_____
A little (-)	_____

3 Choose the correct alternative.

It's *rather / slightly /(extremely)* hot today. It's 40°C.
1 It was sometimes *a bit / really / exceptionally* cold in Tibet. It was only 8°C.
2 I didn't travel by bus much in India. The buses were usually *absolutely / pretty / slightly* full. There were only one or two empty seats.
3 I was in a Brazilian jungle and I wanted something to eat but all the tins were *pretty / a bit / completely* empty. There was nothing left in them at all.
4 I was *slightly / really / a bit* hungry. It was 6 o'clock and I hadn't had anything to eat since breakfast.
5 The train left five minutes late, so we were *extremely / slightly / very* late when we arrived home.

4 Make sentences with the adverbs and the adjectives. Compare your ideas.

very / interesting
I saw a very interesting film on TV last night.
1 really / amazing
2 absolutely / freezing
3 a bit / worried
4 exceptionally / beautiful
5 pretty / poor

LISTENING

5 Listen to Hannah talking to her friend Emily. Answer the questions.
1 Where is Hannah?
2 Is she enjoying herself?
3 Does Emily want to go there?

6 Listen again. Are the sentences true or false?
1 The temperature today is 37°C. ☐ 1
2 The countryside is very different to England. ☐ 2
3 Emily has been to the USA. ☐ 3
4 Canada is not as dangerous as the USA. ☐ 4
5 Hannah doesn't like the people in Canada. ☐ 5
6 Hannah is coming home later this month. ☐ 6

SPEAKING

7 Imagine some foreigners are visiting your country for the first time. Think about what their first impressions would be. Make notes. Include things in these categories.

Food	People	Countryside	Cities	Climate

Food: *lots of meat and rice dishes, main meal in the evening …*

8 Listen and repeat the useful phrases. Pay special attention to your intonation.

Useful phrases
What do you think?   Do you agree?   Why not?
I think …   If you ask me …   In my opinion …
I (don't) agree.   That's (not) true.   You're right.

9 Discuss your ideas from Exercise 1 in pairs. Use the phrases and the example to help you.

A *Let's talk about food. I think that visitors to our country would notice that there are lots of meat and rice dishes.*
B *I agree, and I also think …*

WRITING

INFORMAL LETTERS

1 Beth (18) is from Manchester in England and she's studying in the USA for a year. She's going to write a letter to a friend. Answer the questions.
   a Who is going to read her letter?
   b Will her letter be formal or informal?

2 Read the letter Beth wrote and check your answers.

Dear Richard,

Thanks for your letter. I got it yesterday and I really enjoyed reading it.

California is fantastic! I'm staying with an American family. They're really nice although they say I speak English with a strange accent. It's fairly near the beach so I go there more or less every day after school.

Los Angeles is absolutely enormous. Some areas are very poor and a bit frightening. Other parts are really beautiful, but you have to be extremely rich to live there. One day, maybe ...

What's happening at home? Is it raining as usual? It never rains here. It's hot and sunny every day. I don't want to come home – yet!

Thinking of you all. Write again soon.
Love
Beth

3 Read the letter again and complete the table. Find at least one more expression for each category.

INFORMAL LETTERS	
Opening	**Closing**
Hi! Great to hear from you.	Looking forward to getting your next letter.
	Bye for now.

4 Imagine you're away from home, on holiday. You are going to write a letter to a friend. First make notes. Use the paragraph plan to help you.

> **Paragraph 1:** Start the letter. Thank your friend for his / her letter.
> How long is it since you received your friend's letter?
>
> **Paragraph 2:** Describe what you are doing now and what you do every day.
> Who are you with and where are you staying?
> What do you do during the day and in the evenings?
>
> **Paragraph 3:** Conclude the letter.
> What do you want to ask your friend?
> How are you going to finish your letter?

5 Look at your notes again. Think about the language you will use. Answer the questions.

What expressions will you use to start and finish your letter? (Look at Exercise 3 again.)
What tenses will you use to talk about the past, present and future?
What vocabulary will you need? (Compound nouns? Adverbs of degree?)

6 Write your letter. Write about 120–150 words.

Unit 1

2 A job for life

INTRODUCTION

1 Match the jobs with the pictures.

> nurse   engineer   architect   postman
> grocer   mechanic   hairdresser

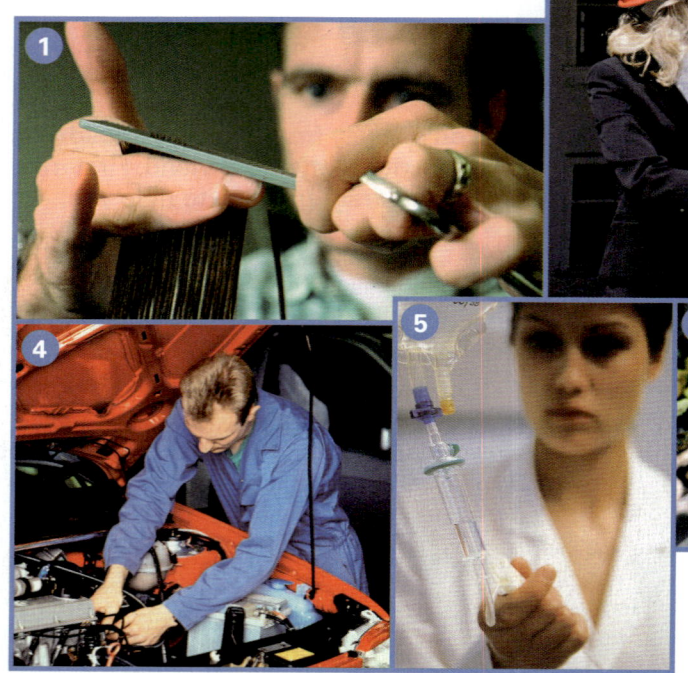

2 Discuss the questions.
1 Would you like to do any of the jobs? Why / Why not?
2 Which of the jobs has the highest status?
3 Which is the most useful to society?
4 Which is the best / worst paid?
5 Which should be the best paid? Why?

READING

3 Read the text quickly. Match the pictures (1–3) with the paragraphs (A–C).

4 Read the text again and answer the questions.
1 When exactly do a lot of British students work?
2 What do most British parents think about their children having a holiday job?
3 What do most British students think about having a job?
4 Why doesn't Alex White work during term time?
5 Why was Jodie able to get a suntan and have a job?
6 Why did Tim and Dan decide to get a job?

5 Match the words from the text with the definitions.
1 survey (line 1)   5 complained (line 20)
2 apparently (line 5)   6 tips (line 24)
3 deliver (line 15)   7 exhausted (line 28)
4 mind (line 17)   8 ladder (line 31)

a a small amount of extra money
b object to or feel upset about something
c extremely tired
d according to what people say
e a piece of equipment that you use for climbing higher
f said that you were not satisfied with something
g to take something to a place or an address
h a study of something

DISCUSSION

6 1 Which of the jobs mentioned in the text would you most / least like to have?
2 Do students in your country get summer jobs? Why / Why not?
3 Have you ever had any kind of job? What did you do? Did you enjoy it? Why / Why not?
4 Do you think it's a good idea for students to have jobs? Why / Why not?

12   Unit 2

Students at work

Who says British students are lazy? A recent survey of typical 15–18 year-old students found that 35% of them had part-time jobs during the school term – usually a Saturday job. In addition, 62% had a full-time job during the school holidays. Did it make any difference if they came from a rich or poor family? Apparently not. Almost all parents wanted their children to get a job, any job, because they could learn a lot from the experience. In particular, they could learn the value of money when they had to earn it by working. And students themselves wanted to work because it gave them a feeling of independence. They also enjoyed having their own money to spend on whatever they liked. Some typical students told us about the jobs they had done.

Alex White

A 'When I was 14 I got a job as a newspaper boy. I had to get up at six o'clock and deliver newspapers to all the houses in our village before starting school at nine. I didn't mind getting up early, but one day I fell asleep while we were doing a Maths test and the teacher noticed. He phoned my parents and complained that I was obviously not getting enough sleep. Now I only work during the school holidays.'

Jodie England

B 'Last summer I got a job as a waitress. The best thing about the job, apart from the tips, was the fact that the restaurant was on the coast, so when it closed after lunch I was free to go to the beach. I lay there all afternoon until it was time to start work again at six o'clock. By the end of the evening, after I had worked non-stop for six hours, I was absolutely exhausted, but that was OK because I didn't start work till twelve the next day.'

Tim Shaw

C 'Last summer my friend Dan and I were complaining about money, or rather the fact that we didn't have any. So we got a ladder, buckets of water and some sponges and started cleaning windows. It was hard work but it paid well, and it was fascinating looking at the inside of some people's houses!'

Unit 2

GRAMMAR

PAST SIMPLE AND PAST CONTINUOUS

1 Read the sentences. Which verbs are in the past simple and which are in the past continuous?
  a When I **was** 14 I **got** a job as a newspaper boy.
  b Last summer my friend Dan and I **were complaining** about money.
  c I **didn't mind** getting up early.
  d I **fell** asleep while we **were doing** a Maths test.

2 Complete the rules with *past simple* or *past continuous*.

> 1 We use the P.S to talk about completed events or actions in the past.
> 2 We use the P.C to talk about something that was in progress at a certain time in the past.
> 3 When we talk about the past, we often use the P.C after *while* and the P.S after *when*.

3 Complete the sentences. Use the past simple or the past continuous.

I (wait) *was waiting* for the bus when it (start) *started* to rain.
  1 I (not work) didn't go to work last Saturday because I (be) was ill.
  2 My boss (come) came in while I (talk) was talking on the phone.
  3 When I (leave) leaved home, the sun (shine) was shining.
  4 It (not rain) was not raining when I (get) got to work.
  5 I (have) had a cup of coffee while (do) was doing my work.
  6 What you (do) did do at nine o'clock yesterday when I (phone) was phoning you?

4 Write one sentence about what you were doing at these times yesterday and another sentence about what you did next.

> At 7.30 yesterday I <u>was having</u> breakfast. After that I <u>left</u> home and <u>came</u> to school.

  1 At 8.00 yesterday I was sleeping After that I had breakfast
  2 At 12.30 yesterday I was studying After that I had lunch
  3 At 6.00 yesterday, I was watching TV. After that I had snack.
  4 At 9.30 yesterday I was surfing net After that I had dinner

5 Work in pairs. Ask and answer questions about what you were doing yesterday.

> *What were you doing at 8 o'clock yesterday?*
> *What did you do after that?*

PAST PERFECT

6 Read the sentences and answer the questions.
  a Some typical students **told** us about the jobs they **had done**.
  b After I **had worked** for six hours, I **was** exhausted.

  1 Which verbs are in the past perfect and which are in the past simple?
  2 When there are two actions, which tense do we normally use for the action that happened first?

7 Complete the text. Use the correct form of the past simple or the past perfect.

I (be) *had been* on holiday from school for a week when I (1 decide) decided to get a job as a waiter. Two days later I (2 get) got a job in a café. I (3 not work) hadn't worked full-time before. At the end of my first day I (4 come) came home and (5 tell) told my parents how hard I (6 work) had worked. Then, as soon as I (7 eat) ate my supper, I (8 go) went to bed!

8 Join the sentences together. Use one verb in the past simple, and one verb in the past perfect.

> Joe got up. He had a shower. (after)
> *After Joe had got up, he had a shower.*

  1 Nick worked for four hours. He had a break. (after) After
  2 Steve wasn't in the office. He went to a conference. (because) because
  3 I went to work. I finished breakfast. (when) when
  4 Simon was tired. He got up early. (because) because
  5 I finished my work in the café. I had a meal. (when) when
  6 The manager went out of the room. We relaxed. (as soon as) as soon as

Grammar reference page 100

Vocabulary

Adjectives of Character

1 Match the pairs of sentences.

1. You're very **considerate**.
2. I'm very **reliable**.
3. You're so **narrow-minded**.
4. You're really **imaginative**.
5. I'm not **mean**.
6. Don't be so **obstinate**.
7. I'm very **determined**.
8. Why aren't you more **ambitious**?

a. You're always coming up with new ideas.
b. You never like new ideas.
c. I just can't afford to pay for it.
d. Thanks for thinking of me.
e. You really can trust me.
f. Nothing's going to stop me now.
g. Don't you want to succeed?
h. It's not too late to change your mind.

2 Complete the table. Use the adjectives from Exercise 1.

Positive meanings	Negative meanings
considerable	ambitious
determined	narrow-minded
considerate	

3 Complete the sentences. Use adjectives from Exercise 1.
1. Adam's being very _____. Can you try to persuade him to change his mind?
2. Sarah's grandparents are very _____. They never accept other people's opinions.
3. Kim's very _____. She's always got lots of really good ideas.
4. Jake lost his job because he wasn't _____ enough. Sometimes he came to work, and sometimes he didn't bother.
5. Joe's making a big effort to get fit. He's _____ to win the 1,500m race next month.
6. Don't be so _____. You can't expect other people to always pay for you.
7. Steve's _____. He wants to get a top job and he won't let anyone stop him.
8. He's not very _____. He only thinks of himself.

4 Complete the text. Use adjectives from Exercise 1.

Vicky Tanner spent several summer holidays working for a travel agency. She met lots of people ...

I liked most of the people I worked with, but there were a few people that I didn't get on with. One or two were (1) _____ – they wouldn't accept any new or different ideas. I tried to talk to them but they were too (2) _____ to change at all. There were also one or two customers who were a bit (3) _____. They complained about the price of everything.

We worked well as a team. Everyone was (4) _____ – you could depend on them to be there at the right time. Most of them were also very (5) _____ with older customers and gave them a lot of extra help. The manager of the company was really (6) _____. He had lots of good ideas to help solve problems. He was also (7) _____ and he always made sure he got what he wanted. I think it's fine to be (8) _____ and to want to succeed if you're kind to other people at the same time.

5 Complete the sentences with adjectives from Exercise 1. Then add another sentence.

I'm very ambitious. I want to get a good, well-paid job.

1. I'm quite ...
2. One of my friends is not very ...
3. My friends say I'm a bit ...
4. I'd like to be more ...
5. When I was younger I was really ...
6. My friend _____ is rather ...

Unit 2   15

READING

1. Look at the title of the text and the pictures. What do you think the text is about?

2. Read the text and check your answer.

3. Read the text again and answer the questions.
   1. What was Tom's father's attitude to flying?
   2. What was Tom's hobby when he was a child?
   3. What made Tom decide to become a pilot?
   4. Why didn't Tom get any money for his work at the airfield?
   5. How did he feel when he first flew solo?
   6. How old was he when he got his driver's licence?
   7. Why is Tom studying again?

4. Find the words in the text and choose the correct definition.
   1. wings (line 13)
      A the two large parts at the sides of a plane that make it fly
      B machines that fly
      C the people who fly planes
   2. landed (line 18)
      A flew
      B climbed higher
      C came down onto the ground
   3. solitary (line 22)
      A on your own
      B like a soldier
      C lonely
   4. take over (line 26)
      A take your turn
      B take your chance
      C take control
   5. obsession (line 33)
      A an illness
      B something that fills your mind all the time
      C a full-time job
   6. in your own hands (line 45)
      A your problem
      B your responsibility
      C out of your control

High-flyer

Tom Butler first flew a plane when he was eight, flew solo two days after his 16th birthday and got his pilot's licence three weeks later – one of the youngest qualified pilots ever.

'I had always been interested in flying despite my father's objections. He's a farmer and he's never flown in his life. He used to say to me "We weren't born with wings so we obviously weren't meant to fly." When I was a small boy I used to cycle to the nearest airfield, 20 kilometres away. There I just stood all day and watched as the planes took off and landed. I didn't use to get home until after dark.

The pilots thought it was strange at first, but then they got used to seeing a small, solitary figure watching them. One day a young pilot offered to take me up in his plane. We were flying at 2,000 metres when he suddenly said, "Right, you can take over the controls now." I couldn't believe it – I was only eight but he was letting me fly his plane. I managed not to crash it and after that there was never any doubt. I was absolutely certain I wanted to be a pilot.

Over the next few years my interest in planes became almost an obsession. I spent every weekend and school holiday at the airfield. They gave me jobs to do such as cutting the grass and cleaning the aircraft. I even cleaned the toilets. They didn't use to pay me anything but they took me up for short flights and gave me flying lessons instead. By the time I was 16 I'd flown over 200 hours.

I'll never forget my first solo flight. It's very different being on your own in a plane for the first time. Your life really is in your own hands and my hands were shaking. My first solo landing was very nearly a disaster! Nevertheless, after a few more lessons I got my pilot's licence, when I was 16 years and 22 days old. I didn't get my driver's licence until two years later. Now I'm studying to be a real airline pilot, and my father is finally used to the idea that I'm never going to be a farmer.'

GRAMMAR

USED TO

1 Read the sentence and answer the questions.

I **used to** cycle to the nearest airfield when I was young.
1. Did he cycle to the airport in the past?
2. Does he cycle to the airfield now?

2 Read the sentences and complete the table.

I **used to work** at the airfield.
I **didn't use to get** home until after dark.
Did they **use to pay** him? No, they **didn't**.

USED TO			
Positive	Negative	Question	Short answer
He used to fly	He _____ fly.	_____ fly?	Yes, _____ / No, _____ .

3 Complete the dialogue. Use *used to* or *didn't use to*. Then practise the dialogue in pairs.

Journalist	Where / you / live? *Where did you use to live?*
Tom	I / live / 20 km from an airfield.
Journalist	How / you / get to the airfield?
Tom	I / cycle.
Journalist	When / you / get home?
Tom	I / get home until after dark.
Journalist	How often / you / go there?
Tom	I / go there / every weekend.
Journalist	What kind of jobs / you / do?
Tom	I / cut the grass.
Journalist	How much / they / pay you?
Tom	They / not pay / me anything.

NOTE!
We can also use *would* to talk about past habits.
I used to cycle to the airfield. OR *I would cycle to the airfield.*

GET USED TO / BE USED TO

4 Read the sentences and answer the questions.
a The pilots **got used to** seeing me there.
b My father **is used to** the idea that I'm never going to be a farmer.

1. Did the pilots think it was unusual when they first saw Tom at the airfield?
2. Did they continue to think it was unusual?
3. Does Tom's father now accept that he doesn't want to be a farmer?
4. Did he accept it at first?

5 Complete the rules. Use *get* and *be*.
1. We use _____ + *used to* when something strange is becoming normal.
2. We use _____ + *used to* when something isn't strange any more. It's now normal.

6 Joanna is talking about her new job. Complete the text. Use a correct form of *be used to* or *get used to*.

When I started my job I *wasn't used to* getting up at 6.45 a.m. in order to take the bus to work. I found it hard to (1) _____ travelling to work, too. When I was a student I didn't have to travel as far. Also when I was at university I (2) _____ having two hours for lunch between classes. It has taken me a long time to (3) _____ only having half an hour for lunch. And I'm still (4) _____ wearing smart clothes. I never wore a suit when I was a student! However, there are some good things about my new job. I've (5) _____ having more money and I've also (6) _____ spending lots of money on new clothes, which I love!

7 Complete the sentences about yourself.
1. Five years ago I wasn't used to …
2. These days I'm getting used to …
3. I'm also used to …
4. But I'm still not used to …

Grammar reference page 100

Unit 2 17

VOCABULARY

THE WORLD OF WORK

1 Read the text and answer the questions.

I'm still at school and I don't know what I'm going to do for a **career** yet. Last summer I got a job in a clothes shop. It wasn't a **full-time** job. I only wanted to work four days a week so that I could spend time with my friends. The manager gave me a bit of training on my first day but after that I was on my own, although I didn't have to **run** the whole shop. I was just **in charge of** the jeans department. I was good at my job and I got on well with the **customers**, so I asked the manager for a **pay rise**. He wasn't paying me nearly enough! But he refused, so a week later I **gave in my notice**. After that I was **unemployed** till I went back to school. But I wasn't worried because I had earned enough money to go out every evening with my friends.

1 Has Kate chosen her future career?
2 Why didn't Kate want a full-time job?
3 Who ran the whole shop?
4 Who was in charge of the jeans department?
5 Did Kate like the customers?
6 Why did she ask for a pay rise?
7 Why did she decide to give in her notice?
8 What did she do when she became unemployed?

2 Complete the sentences. Use the words in bold in Exercise 1.

1 'Was it a _____ job?' 'No, I only worked at weekends.'
2 My sister doesn't just want a badly paid temporary job. She wants a real _____ .
3 Our neighbour lost his job six months ago and since then he's been _____ .
4 You must always smile and be polite to _____ , even when they're rude to you.
5 I worked for a month and then I _____ . I didn't want to work there any longer.
6 I got a _____ yesterday! I now earn £250 a week.
7 I'm not _____ anything. My boss makes all the decisions.
8 Two managers _____ the whole department.

LISTENING

3 Listen to the interviews. What are the two jobs?

4 Listen again and complete the table. Who was offered the job?

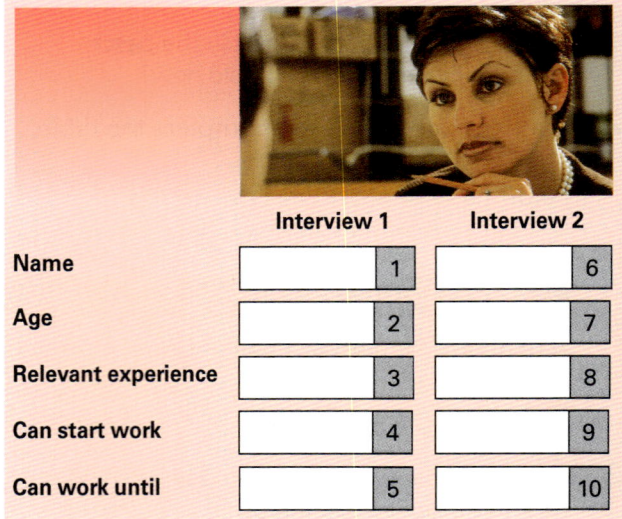

	Interview 1	Interview 2
Name	1	6
Age	2	7
Relevant experience	3	8
Can start work	4	9
Can work until	5	10

SPEAKING

5 You are going to prepare a job interview. Work in groups. Ask and answer the questions about each job.

> a football player   a businessman   a TV presenter

1 What sort of person do you need to be?
2 What experience do you need?
3 What qualifications do you need?
A *I think you need to be ambitious to be a top football player.*
B *I don't think that's true. You just have to be very good at football.*

6 Work in pairs. Choose one of the jobs from Exercise 5 or another job. Prepare questions and answers for a job interview.

Student A: You are going to interview Student B. Prepare questions. Use the ideas in Exercises 4 and 5 to help you.

Why do you think you'd be good at this job?
What qualifications have you got?

Student B: Student A is going to interview you for a job. Think of reasons why you want the job and why you would be good at it. Prepare questions to ask student A about the job.

I think I'd be good at this job because ...
What are the main responsibilities of this job?

7 Role play the job interview.

18   Unit 2

WRITING

BRAINSTORMING IDEAS

1. Plan your writing. Look at this student's mind map.

2. Read the essay. Which ideas from the mind map have been included?

> **What job do you think you'd be good at and why?**
>
> I've often thought about what type of job I want to do after I leave school. I used to want to be a farmer like my father, but last year I changed my mind. I think I want to be an architect, now.
>
> I think I'd be good at the job for many reasons. I'm good at maths and art. I enjoy solving technical problems, too. I've also decided that I don't like working outside like my father, especially in the winter. I'd prefer to work inside, in a warm office. I'd like to earn quite a lot of money as well, much more than a farmer!
>
> Now that I've made my decision I'm getting used to the idea that the training will take a long time. However I think it will lead to a very interesting career.

3. Brainstorm your own ideas. Make a mind map for the essay topic *'What job do you think you'd be good at and why?'*

4. Write an essay of 120–150 words using your best ideas from Exercise 3. Use the paragraph plan to help you.

> Paragraph 1: A general introduction and the job you've chosen.
> Paragraph 2: At least three reasons why you think you'd be good at the job.
> Paragraph 3: A conclusion.

Unit 2   **19**

Units 1–2: revision

GRAMMAR

REVIEW OF TENSES

1 Complete the text. Use the present simple, present continuous, past simple or past continuous.

> Paco Alvarez (play) *plays* football for Bangor, in North Wales. Paco is Argentinian. He (1 come) _____ from Buenos Aries. At the moment he (2 play) _____ snooker, but later in the evening a friend of his (3 come) _____ to his flat and they (4 go) _____ to a Chinese restaurant together.
>
> On the day Paco first (5 arrive) _____ in Wales it (6 snow) _____ , a cold wind (7 blow) _____ and he definitely (8 not want) _____ to stay. But now, nine months later, he (9 enjoy) _____ himself and he (10 not want) _____ to go home to Argentina.

2 Write sentences. Use the present simple, present continuous, past simple or past continuous.

Ana / study / English in London.
Ana is studying English in London.

1 She / come / to Britain two months ago.
2 When she first / arrive / she / not understand / much English.
3 Her English / get / better now but she still / not understand / everything.
4 She / have / lots of English friends and she / go out with / some of them this evening.
5 She / meet / them last week when she / sit / in a café.
6 She / do / her homework in the café and they / offer / to help her.

3 Complete the sentences. Use the past perfect.

Lucy (see) *had seen* the film before.
1 When I got home everybody (go) _____ to bed.
2 Nathan told us a joke which we (not hear) _____ before.
3 The concert (start) _____ when we arrived.
4 We (not meet) _____ since we were at school together.
5 I didn't go out until I (finish) _____ my homework.
6 Mahmut (not speak) _____ much English before he went to England.

GERUNDS

4 Complete the text. Use the gerund forms of the words in the box.

> ~~go~~   find   leave   travel   keep   arrive   worry   show   start

> I love *going* abroad and last summer I went to Paris with a friend. Before (1) _____ , I got a new passport. My old passport had a terrible photo of me in it, so I didn't like (2) _____ it to anyone.
>
> We went to Paris by train. Normally I enjoy (3) _____ by train, but (4) _____ a seat on that train was impossible because it was so full. (5) _____ in Paris by train for the first time was very exciting, but before (6) _____ to explore I sent my parents an email from an Internet café. I'm 18 but they can't help (7) _____ about me and (8) _____ in touch by email is so easy.

USED TO, BE / GET USED TO

5 Match the two parts of the sentences.

1 Nick used to live in a small village
2 He wasn't used to living in a big city
3 He's getting used to it now
4 Before, when he lived at home,
5 Now he's used to
6 But he'll never

a because he's lived there for six months.
b his mother always used to cook for him.
c but now he lives in London.
d get used to washing his own clothes.
e so he found it strange at first.
f cooking for himself.

20 Revision 1–2

VOCABULARY

COMPOUND NOUNS

1 Answer the questions.

1. Why do many people need an alarm clock?
2. Why are girls more likely to use a hairdryer than boys?
3. Where do you normally find a tin opener?
4. What can you do with a penknife?
5. Why is a laptop computer sometimes more useful than a desktop computer?
6. Which would you prefer to have – a CD player or a coffee maker? Why?
7. Why is a washing machine so useful?
8. What are the advantages and disadvantages of having a credit card?
9. Who usually pays the bills if a teenager has a mobile phone?

ADVERBS OF DEGREE

2 Choose the correct alternative.

It was (1) *extremely / fairly / a bit* hot when I first arrived in India. The temperature was 48 degrees. For breakfast I had my first curry. It was (2) *slightly / really / a bit* hot. I had to drink a litre of water with it – and I only ate three mouthfuls! At the end of the first day I was (3) *totally / rather / fairly* exhausted. I couldn't walk another step. Finding cheap accommodation was (4) *fairly / extremely / exceptionally* easy. It only took me half an hour. The hostel was (5) *fairly / completely / pretty* empty. There was nobody staying there at all. But my bed was (6) *extremely / a bit / rather* uncomfortable. I didn't sleep at all.

ADJECTIVES OF CHARACTER

3 Complete the sentences to show that you understand the adjectives of character.

My grandfather is very **narrow-minded**. *He's never interested in other people's opinions.*

1. Don't be so **impatient**. We …
2. Why are you so **obstinate**? Why can't you … ?
3. He's very **reliable** so you can be sure …
4. I'm not **mean**. I …
5. She's very **ambitious**. She wants …
6. You're being very **selfish**. Why don't you … ?
7. She's not very **imaginative**. She never …
8. He wasn't very **considerate**. He always …
9. She's a very **determined** person who wants …

THE WORLD OF WORK

4 Complete the text with the words and phrases in the box.

> full time   run   unemployed   career   customers
> in charge of   pay rise   give in her notice

When she was 16 my sister Lisa decided that she wanted to be a hairdresser. My father was very upset. He didn't think hairdressing was a real (1) ____. He wanted her to get some qualifications and a job which led somewhere. But Lisa didn't want to stay on at school. She wanted to (2) ____ her own hairdressing salon and be (3) ____ at least ten other hairdressers. So as soon as she left school she began working in a local hairdresser's. She worked (4) ____, sometimes as many as 48 hours a week, and she was very good at talking to (5) ____ . She worked there for a year but when she didn't get a (6) ____ she decided to (7) ____ and a week later she left. Now Lisa's (8) ____ and I don't know what she's going to do.

> Now look at the song on page 94.

Revision 1–2   **21**

3 Teenage blues

INTRODUCTION

1 Which of the statements do you agree with? Discuss your answers in groups.
1 The teenage years are the best years of your life.
2 Teenagers have more to worry about than adults.
3 Today's teenagers are often confused because they have to make so many choices.
4 It's important to decide what job you want to do as soon as possible.

READING

2 Read the text. What is it about? Choose the correct alternative.
A The advantages of being a teenager today.
B It's fun being young.
C The pressures on today's teenagers.

3 Read the text again. For questions 1–5 choose the correct answer A, B, or C.
1 According to the text, adults think that
   A it's difficult being a teenager.
   B adults enjoy themselves more than teenagers.
   C it's fun to be young.
2 Jenny Harvey says that
   A adults work harder than teenagers.
   B teenagers work harder than adults.
   C teenagers have plenty of free time.
3 According to the text, which is the most important?
   A Being good-looking.
   B Going to parties.
   C Belonging to a group.
4 Jamie Evans says his parents want him to
   A make his own choices.
   B have the best opportunities.
   C go to university.
5 How do most teenagers feel about the future?
   A They're uncertain.
   B They're excited.
   C They're unconcerned.

4 Find words in the text with similar meanings to:
1 stresses (paragraph A)
2 worry (paragraph B)
3 a rest (paragraph B)
4 strong and fearless (paragraph C)
5 frightening (paragraph E)
6 choices (paragraph E)

5 Explain the meaning of the phrases.
1 a laugh a minute (line 4)
2 the end of the world (line 13)
3 they can switch off (line 18)
4 hang out with the right people (line 31)
5 Time is on our side (line 68)

DISCUSSION

6 Discuss the questions.
1 What sort of pressures are you under at school and at home?
2 How much time do you spend on average on homework?
3 How important do you think it is to pass exams?
4 Do you want to go to university? Why / Why not?

22   Unit 3

The best years?

A Adults often say, 'It's great when you're young – they're the best years of your life. Enjoy them while you can.' But being a teenager isn't a laugh a minute. School, work, your parents, the way you look, who your friends are – these are just some of the pressures which adults seem to forget about.

B Perhaps the biggest cause of anxiety is the need to do well at school. Exams are becoming more and more important, and sometimes people seem to think it's the end of the world if you don't pass every exam you take with top marks. 'It's much easier being an adult,' says Jenny Harvey (16). 'When they come home from work, they can switch off and take it easy. They're much freer than us. We have to do our homework, study for tests and revise for exams. We never get a break!'

C When you're young, it's also important to be popular. For some that's easy. The most popular boys are usually good at sport or tough. For girls, the emphasis is on looks and clothes. But being popular isn't always as important as just belonging to a group – any group. According to Emily Collins (18), 'That's one of the hardest things about being a teenager. If you don't hang out with the right people, you don't get invited to parties, you sit on your own in class, nobody sends you text messages and you just feel lonely.'

D What about parents? Do they put pressure on you as well? 'My parents get worried when I get home late or spend a lot of time with my friends during the week,' says Jamie Evans (17). 'They also insist that I work hard.' 'They want me to do well at school because they think that a good education will give me more choices later on in life.'

E In fact today's teenagers have to make more choices than ever before, and those choices are getting harder and harder. As a result teenagers are often more confused and less confident. It's difficult to decide which subjects to study, whether to get a job or go to university, particularly when most teenagers have no idea about what they want to do or be in the future. 'There are so many options that it's scary,' admits Jamie. 'When you're an adult, your life is kind of decided for you. We're still deciding. But perhaps that's the best thing about being young. We've got it all before us so it doesn't matter if we make a few mistakes. Time is on our side.'

Unit 3   23

GRAMMAR

COMPARATIVES AND SUPERLATIVES

1 Read the sentences. How is the comparative and superlative of *hard* formed?

Those choices are getting **harder**.
That's the **hardest** thing about being a teenager.

2 Match the words with the ways of forming comparatives and superlatives.

| faster / fastest   bigger / biggest   easier / easiest |
| larger / largest   more difficult / most difficult |
| worse / worst |

1 add -*r* and -*st*
2 add -*er* and -*est*
3 add *more* and *most*
4 use completely different words
5 change spelling and add -*ier* and –*iest*
6 double the final consonant and add -*er* and -*est*

NOTE!

With long adjectives we can use *less* and *least*. These are the opposites of *more* and *most*.
English exams are less difficult than Maths exams.
Texting is the least expensive way to communicate.

3 Read the sentences and complete the rules.
1 metre is **as** long **as** 100 centimetres.
Cassettes are **not as** expensive **as** CDs.

We use _____ + adjective + _____ to compare two things that are similar.

We can use not _____ + adjective + _____ to compare two things that are different.

4 Rewrite the sentences. Use comparatives, (*not*) *as* + *as* or superlatives.

The radio is less entertaining than the TV. (not / interesting)
The radio *is not as interesting as* the TV.

1 Cola is more expensive than tea. (cheap)
  Tea …
2 Having good looks isn't as essential as belonging to a group. (important)
  Belonging to a group …
3 Doing homework and revising for exams are both hard things to do. (difficult)
  Revising for exams …
4 There is no better way to spend an evening than meeting my friends. (enjoyable)
  Meeting my friends …
5 Adults have more confidence than teenagers. (not / confident)
  Teenagers …

5 Discuss the questions.
1 What's the hardest and easiest choice you have made this week?
2 What's the best and the worst thing about being a teenager?
3 Are the pressures on teenagers as serious as the text on page 23 suggests?

OTHER COMPARATIVE FORMS

6 Look at the sentences and the words in the box. Which words mean the same as *much*? Which words mean the same as *a bit*?

| a lot   far   slightly   a little |

It's **a bit** easier being an adult than being a teenager.
Adults are **much** freer than teenagers.

7 Look at the example and complete the text. Choose from the words in the box.

| ~~a lot / cheap~~   a bit / fast   much / popular |
| a little / long   far / few   far / common |

Mobile phones used to be expensive but today they're getting *a lot cheaper*. As a result they're quickly becoming (1) _____ on city streets. Teenagers especially love small phones with lots of gadgets. These phones are (2) _____ than standard mobiles – especially with teenagers.

Many young people send text messages too. It's a cheaper way to communicate, although it takes (3) _____ . When they want to send a message (4) _____ they often use abbreviations for common words. One result of people using mobiles is that there are (5) _____ public telephones in the street nowadays.

Grammar reference page 102

24   Unit 3

VOCABULARY

EDUCATION: VERB + NOUN

1 Look at the examples of verb + noun. For questions 1–5, which verbs can you not use with each of the nouns?

It's the end of the world if you don't **pass** every **exam**.

We have to **do homework**.

Today's teenagers have to **make** more **choices** than ever before.

It's difficult to decide which **subjects** to **study**.

It's hard to decide or not whether to **go** to **university**.

You can _____ a question.
A write
B ask
C think (circled)
D answer

1 You can _____ an exam.
A take
B fail
C revise for
D get

2 You can _____ a subject.
A choose
B study
C have
D drop

3 You can _____ homework.
A do
B make
C get
D finish

4 You can _____ a choice.
A make
B have
C offer
D decide

5 You can _____ university.
A go to
B get into
C do
D study at

2 Complete the text. Use the correct form of the verbs in the box.

| study | get into | fail | drop | take | ~~do~~ | pass |
| have | revise | make | go to | | | |

I'm doing my homework, as usual. At the moment I (1) _____ for some important exams which I (2) _____ next week. It's important that I (3) _____ them but I'm afraid that I might (4) _____ the maths exam – I'm terrible at Maths. I wish I could (5) _____ Maths but unfortunately everyone has to do it. I (6) _____ no choice.

My parents want me to (7) _____ university but I'm not sure that I'm clever enough to (8) _____ the same university as most of my friends. But if I do, I'll have to (9) _____ a difficult choice and decide which subject I want to (10) _____ . It definitely won't be Maths!

3 Complete the sentences. Use the words in brackets to help you.

We need to study in the evenings (pass / exams) *to pass our exams.*

1 I finish homework (answer / questions) …
2 I revise for exams (get / good mark) …
3 We take exams (check / understanding) …
4 We have to make choices (get into / university) …
5 Many students go to university (study / subject) …
6 To get into university (take / exam) …

Unit 3   25

READING

1 Read the text and answer the question.

1 Why is the story called 'The last laugh'?

The last laugh

Emma didn't have much time. She had a sick feeling in her stomach but she had to go to school – there was no getting out of it. 'Bye mum,' she shouted as she put a few books into her bag and left the house.

5 It was a grey day and it started to rain as she quickly walked towards the bus stop. 'Hey Emma! Wait for me!' a voice called from behind. It was Zoe, running to catch up. 'Thanks for helping me out yesterday,' she said, pulling her coat around her shoulders. 'Not many people turn against Anna – they're
10 too scared. None of my other friends dared.' 'That's OK,' said Emma, trying not to feel irritated. She couldn't admit to Zoe how much she was now regretting it. She was already under enough pressure at school without making enemies of people like Anna. Why hadn't she just kept quiet and walked away?
15 'Aren't you worried about what she'll do?' asked Zoe. 'No,' said Emma coolly. 'I can take care of myself.'

The morning was uneventful. There was no sign of Anna or any of her friends. 'Perhaps she isn't in today,' thought Emma, feeling relieved …

20 It was midday and the school bell rang for lunch. Emma went down to the canteen. She noticed Zoe at a nearby table, but she pretended she hadn't seen her and sat on her own. Emma had some sandwiches, a few biscuits and some orange juice, but she wasn't feeling hungry. 'Well, look who it is!' someone
25 said suddenly. Emma froze, then slowly looked behind her. It was Anna with several of her friends. They were standing there, just staring at her. 'Get lost,' said Emma and carried on eating. Anna walked past, looked down at her and then deliberately knocked Emma's sandwiches onto the floor.
30 'Oops, you're not having much luck today, are you?' she said as she carried on walking, at the same time carefully treading the sandwiches into the floor. Emma was furious, but there was nothing she could do.

Then something extraordinary happened. As Anna turned to
35 walk away she slipped on one of the sandwiches. Emma looked up just in time to see her crash into Zoe's table and fall into a plate of spaghetti. Everyone was pointing and laughing as Anna got up, red with embarrassment, and covered in sauce. 'Would you like some parmesan cheese with that?' said
40 Zoe, smiling innocently …

2 Read the text again and answer the questions.

1 Why did Emma have a sick feeling in her stomach?
2 What did she now regret?
3 Why did she feel relieved that morning?
4 Why did Anna knock Emma's sandwiches onto the floor?
5 How did Emma react?
6 Why did everyone laugh at Anna?

3 Match the words from the text with the definitions.

1 regretting   a when nothing important happens
2 uneventful   b behaved in a certain way to deceive someone.
3 pretended   c pressing something down with your foot
4 deliberately
5 treading   d feeling sorry about something you did
6 furious   e all around someone or something
7 surrounded   f as if you have done nothing wrong
8 innocently   g very angry
                       h on purpose; not by accident

4 Explain the meaning of the phrases.

1 There was no getting out of it. (line 2)
2 I can take care of myself. (line 16)
3 no sign of (line 17)
4 just in time (line 36)

DISCUSSION

5 Discuss the questions.

1 Why do you think some teenagers are bullies?
2 What sort of people do they usually bully?
3 What is the best way to stop being bullied?

26 Unit 3

GRAMMAR

QUANTIFIERS

1 Look at the sentences and complete the table. Use the words in the box.

She put **a few** books into her bag.

'You're not having **much** luck today, are you?'

She had **some** sandwiches … and **some** orange juice for lunch.

| many   most of   much   a little   a few   several |
| a lot of   plenty of   a bit of   most   some   any |
| more   enough   none of   all of |

COUNTABLE AND UNCOUNTABLE NOUNS

Countable	Uncountable	Countable and uncountable
many		

NOTE!
Some quantifiers are mainly used in positive sentences: *a little, a few, several, plenty of, a bit, some, none of*. Some quantifiers are mainly used in negative sentences: *much, any*.

2 Choose the correct alternative.

In the mornings, Emma puts (1) *a bit of / a few* books in her bag and goes to school. She hasn't got (2) *many / a few* friends so at lunchtime she often sits on her own. She only takes (3) *a few / not many* minutes to eat her lunch – she normally has (4) *some / a little* sandwiches with (5) *any / a bit of* cheese or egg in them. Then she goes back to the school library. She spends (6) *much / a little* time there every day. She reads (7) *several / much* books every week. She hasn't got (8) *many / much* money so she can't afford to buy (9) *none / many* of them.

3 Rewrite the sentences. Use words from Exercise 1 with similar meanings to the words in bold.

Sophie wants to buy a new bag but she hasn't got **a lot** of money.

Sophie wants to buy a new bag but she hasn't got much money.

1 Steve's got **one or two** problems – he finds school work hard and he hasn't got many friends.
2 We've got **more than enough** time. The bus doesn't leave for 10 minutes.
3 **A number of** my friends have got mobiles but not all of them.
4 The exam is next week so you've only got **a bit of** time left to revise.
5 **Not one of** my friends has sent me a text message.
6 **The majority of** the students in my class bring their own sandwiches for lunch.
7 **Not a lot of** people walk to school. They prefer to go by bus.

4 Make sentences about the people. Use words from Exercise 1.

boys / motorbikes: *A lot of boys are interested in motorbikes.*

1 girls / clothes
2 the people in my country / go on holiday
3 my friends / have computers
4 young people / opera
5 the students in my class / want to study English at university

5 Make three more sentences about people you know well. Compare your ideas with other students.

Grammar reference page 102

Unit 3   27

Vocabulary

Phrasal verbs: friendship

1 Read the text and match the phrasal verbs with their meanings below.

Bella was a good friend to Susie, but Susie was very unreliable. She often turned up late and forgot to keep her promises. However Bella (1) **put up with** Susie's faults and never complained. If anyone criticised Susie, Bella always (2) **stuck up for her**. In fact she was always there when Susie needed her, and never (3) **let her down**. Then one day Bella (4) **turned against** Susie. They had a bad argument and (5) **fell out**. Why? Because Susie went out with Bella's ex-boyfriend. Susie tried to (6) **make up** with Bella, but Bella never spoke to her again.

a supported or defended someone
b became unfriendly towards someone
c disappointed someone, didn't keep a promise
d argued and stopped being friends
e became friends with someone again
f tolerated

2 Discuss the questions.
1 Have you ever fallen out with anyone? Were you able to make up later on?
2 Do you put up with things or do you complain about them?
3 Have you ever let anyone down? What happened? Has anyone ever let you down?
4 What TV programmes have you seen where someone has stuck up for a friend, or has turned against someone? What happened?

Listening

3 Listen to three teenagers talking about their best friends. For each speaker, identify the adjectives they use to describe them. Which adjectives describe a) positive and b) negative characteristics?

Speaker 1	funny	☐
	strange	☐
	forgetful	☐
Speaker 2	loyal	☐
	big-headed	☐
	scary	☐
Speaker 3	intelligent	☐
	silly	☐
	shy	☐

4 Listen again and match the speakers with the statements.

Which speaker(s):
1 had a friend who stuck up for him / her?
2 does schoolwork with his / her friend?
3 fell out with his / her friend?
4 goes shopping with his / her friend?
5 plays a sport with his / her friend?
6 puts up with his / her friend's faults?
7 always makes up with his / her friend after an argument?

Speaking

5 What qualities should a good friend have? Look at the list below and add two more things.

A good friend should …
- be popular with other people.
- stick up for you.
- like the same music and wear the same clothes.
- put up with your faults.
- never let you down.
- help you with your homework.
- be able to keep a secret.
- _____
- _____

6 In pairs, choose the three most important qualities from your list. Give reasons for your choice.

7 Compare your list with other students. Try to agree on the same three qualities.

WRITING

LINKING WORDS: TIME SEQUENCERS

1 Read the story and match the pictures with the paragraphs.

The Surprise

1 Enzo wasn't really tall enough to be a good basketball player. He was always the last person to be picked, especially today when they were playing against another school. But one of their best players was ill so the team captain didn't have much choice.

2 The game started and **to begin with** Enzo tried hard, but nobody wanted to pass him the ball. **At first** he was frustrated. Then he got the ball a couple of times but he immediately lost it. **After that** he stopped trying because he didn't want to let his team down. The minutes went by and the score was close. There were only a few tense seconds of the game left.

3 **Then** suddenly something extraordinary happened. The referee looked at his watch, but **before** he could blow his whistle somebody shouted Enzo's name. **When** Enzo looked up, he saw the ball coming towards him. He knew what he had to do. He ran towards the basket and scored! **Finally** the referee blew the whistle and ended the game.

2 Read the story again and answer the questions.
1 Why was Enzo playing in the team?
2 How did he feel at the beginning of the game?
3 What problems did he experience?
4 How did he react?
5 What did he have to do at the end of the game?
6 Why is the story called 'The Surprise'?

3 Look at the words in **bold**. They are used to order events in a story. Which words are used to:
- introduce a sequence of events?
- link two events?
- introduce a final event?

4 Choose the correct answer.
(1) *To begin with / When* Enzo was chosen for the school team, he was very pleased. (2) *Then / At first* he wanted to play well, but nobody passed him the ball. (3) *Then / Before* he started to get angry. (4) *After / Finally* 30 minutes Enzo got the ball, but he lost it immediately! (5) *After that / At first* he stopped playing seriously for a while. However, (6) *then / when* he got the ball at the end of the match, he knew he had to score – and he did! (7) *Finally / Before* the referee blew his whistle and everyone was cheering for Enzo.

5 You are going to write a story about an ordinary day when something extraordinary happened. First answer the questions.
1 Is your story going to be a real story or an imaginary story?
2 Who is telling the story – you or someone else?
3 Did your story happen in school or out of school?
4 What was the event that made the day extraordinary?
5 What happened before, during and after the event?

6 Write your story. Use words from Exercise 4 to order the events, and the paragraph plan to help you. Write 120–150 words.

Paragraph 1:	Describe the situation: where you were, who you were with, and what you were doing. Introduce the main character(s).
Paragraph 2:	Describe what happened to make the day extraordinary.
Paragraph 3:	Describe what happened in the end.

Unit 3   29

4 Taking risks

INTRODUCTION

1 Look at the pictures. What are the people doing?

2 Describe the people in the pictures. Use the words in the box. Give reasons for your choice.

> sensible irresponsible
> selfish determined brave
> adventurous crazy

3 Do you think the activities are dangerous? What could go wrong? What could you do to make these sports safer?

READING

4 Read the sentences and predict the topic of each paragraph.

Paragraph A
Today there aren't many new things left for explorers and risk takers to do.

Paragraph B
38-year-old Davo Karnicar is a typical modern-day adventurer.

Paragraph C
Jim Shekhdar is another adventurer who enjoys unusual challenges.

5 Read the text and check your predictions.

6 Read the text again. Are the sentences true or false?
1 There are no new places for people to explore.
2 Most risk-takers want to do something different.
3 Davo has been interested in climbing for a long time.
4 He first climbed Mount Everest when he was only eight.
5 Davo thinks people who do extreme sports are crazy.
6 Jim Shekhdar had very few people with him when he crossed the Pacific Ocean.
7 He had nightmares about hitting another boat.
8 Rowing across the Pacific is Jim Shekhdar's last adventure.

7 Find the words in the text and choose the correct definition.
1 challenges (line 3)
   A things that are difficult
   B things that are predictable
   C things that are easy
2 a gift (line 22)
   A a natural ability
   B a present
   C an ambition
3 collided (line 30)
   A avoided
   B crashed into
   C sank
4 deterred (line 32)
   A encouraged
   B persuaded
   C discouraged

8 Explain the meaning of the phrases.
1 single-handed (line 6)
2 no way (line 33)

DISCUSSION

9 Discuss the questions.
1 Do you think Davo and Jim are crazy? Why / Why not?
2 How do you think their families feel about their adventures?
3 How would your family feel if you became an explorer?

30 Unit 4

No Limits

Today there aren't many new things left for explorers and risk takers to do. Adventurers are constantly looking for new challenges, but people have already climbed the highest mountains, dived to the bottom of the deepest oceans, walked to the North and South Poles and sailed round the world single-handed. So dedicated risk takers have started to take up weird and wonderful activities. Instead of climbing Everest, they hang-glide off it; instead of trekking to the North Pole they go there by mountain bike. People have travelled round the world using everything from hot-air balloons and microlight planes to motorbikes and camels. But why do they do it?

38-year-old Davo Karnicar is a typical modern-day adventurer. Davo has had a passion for mountains since he was eight years old and recently he climbed Mount Everest. 'That's nothing new,' you might say, but once he got to the top he did something very different – he skied down the other side! It took him one month to climb it, but just five hours to reach the bottom at an amazing 130kph, and of course it's never been done before. 'Everyone has a gift,' he explains. 'I know how to ski. Someone else might know how to drive a Formula 1 car. Does that make us crazy?'

Jim Shekhdar is another adventurer who enjoys unusual challenges. Jim has just finished a journey across the Pacific Ocean – alone and in a rowing boat! It took him 275 days to do it, and during that time he fought off sharks and survived terrible storms. But the worst moment was when a huge cargo ship almost collided with his boat. 'I couldn't sleep for a week after that,' he said. 'It was something that seriously affected me.' So has it deterred him from having more adventures in the future? 'No way!' he laughs. 'Next time I'll try something really difficult!'

'Climber to ski down Everest' by Oliver August. *The Times*, London (6 October 2000). Jim Shekhdar story from *Reuters*.

GRAMMAR

PRESENT PERFECT SIMPLE

1 Match the sentences with the rules.

a Davo **has had** a passion for mountains since he was eight years old.
b I**'ve already prepared** everything for the climb, so we can go now.
c '**Have you ever been** in a hot-air balloon?' 'No, I **haven't**.'

> We can use the present perfect to talk about
> 1 something that started in the past and continues in the present.
> 2 life experiences, when we don't say when they happened.
> 3 something that happened in the past that has a result in the present.

2 Find another example of each use of the present perfect in the text on page 31.

People have already climbed the highest mountains. (line 3)

FOR AND SINCE

3 Read the sentences and complete the rules. Use *for* and *since*.

a Jim hasn't seen another boat **for** days.
b Davo has wanted to climb mountains **since** he was a child.

> 1 We use _____ with a period of time, for example a week, two days.
> 2 We use _____ with a point in time, for example yesterday, last week.

4 Complete the sentences. Use the present perfect tense and *for* or *since*.

Ellen (not won) ____ a sailing competition ___ ages.
Ellen hasn't won a sailing competition for ages.

1 Matt (be) _____ interested in adventure sports _____ he was sixteen.
2 We (not hear) _____ anything about the expedition _____ a long time.
3 I (not be) _____ skiing _____ I broke my leg.
4 Sports like bungee jumping (be) _____ popular _____ years.
5 Bella (have) _____ a surfboard _____ the New Year.
6 The diver (not come up for) _____ air _____ three minutes.

ALREADY, JUST AND YET

5 Read the sentences and complete the rules. Use *already*, *just* or *yet*.

a Tina has **already** learnt how to snowboard.
b Ivan has **just** got to the top of the mountain.
c They haven't finished skiing **yet**.

> We put _____ and _____ after *have / has* and before the past participle.
> We usually put _____ at the end of a sentence. We use it with questions and negatives.

6 Read the interview. Rewrite the sentences. Put the words in the correct order and write the verbs in **bold** in the present perfect tense.

A a snowboarder / how long / **be** / you / ?
How long have you been a snowboarder?
B I / **start** / just /.
A many lessons / you / **have** / ?
B No, I haven't. / since January / two lessons / **have** / I /.
A extreme sports / you / **do** / before / ?
B Yes, I have. / I / already / **be** / bungee jumping several times /.
A a snowboard / yet / you / **buy** / ?
B Yes, one / **get** / I / just /.
A yet / an accident / **have** / you / ?
B No, I haven't. But / some scary experiences / **have** / I /.

7 Complete the questions about sport. Use the present perfect tense and the words to help you.

1 just / start / the sport?
Have you just started playing the sport?
2 how long / do / for?
3 how many / lessons / have?
4 already / buy / equipment?
5 play / competition / yet?
6 ever / have / accident?

8 Work in pairs. Interview each other about a sport you do or imagine you do. Use the questions in Exercise 7.

Grammar reference page 103

32 Unit 4

VOCABULARY

PHRASAL VERBS: LOOK

1 Match the phrasal verbs with the definitions.

1 Simon carefully **looked over** his parachute before he jumped out of the plane.
2 When Jim **looked back on** his experiences at sea, he felt very lucky.
3 When you're climbing you need to **look out for** falling rocks.
4 Hundreds of spectators **looked on** while Davo skied down Everest.
5 Peter **looked up to** Mark. He was a very experienced explorer.
6 The company **looked into** the possibility of sponsoring the *X-Games*.

a watched something happen
b examined or checked something
c respected or admired someone
d thought about things that happened in the past
e investigated something
f was careful of something dangerous

2 Complete the sentences. Use the correct form of the verbs in Exercise 1.

Susie *looked on* while her friend did the bungee jump.

1 During his journey, Jim had to _____ sharks.
2 Sarah _____ the map carefully before she started her journey.
3 The expedition team _____ the reasons why the accident had happened.
4 When John _____ his first sky dive, he remembered feeling nervous. It was a frightening experience!
5 People _____ explorers because of their amazing achievements.

3 Answer the questions.

1 Who do you look up to? Why?
2 Describe an experience you look back on with strong feelings.
3 Have you ever looked into the possibility of doing an unusual sport?
4 What should you look out for when you're driving a car?

ADVENTURE SPORTS

4 Match the pictures with the adventure sports.

windsurfing   abseiling   snowboarding
bungee jumping   sky-diving   hang-gliding

5 Complete the sentences. Use the sports from Exercise 4.

1 _____ is a jump from a plane with a parachute.
2 Tina loves _____ . It's a challenge to go down a mountain slowly controlling a rope.
3 Mark is good at _____ . It's similar to surfing, but with a sail.
4 Despite the danger, many people still go _____ off bridges and buildings.
5 Nowadays you can go _____ or skiing at ski resorts.
6 _____ can be a dangerous sport as the aircraft has no engine.

6 Discuss the questions.

Which of these sports would you like to try? Which would you not like to try? Give reasons for your answers.

Unit 4   33

READING

1 Read the text. What is it about? Choose the best alternative.
- A A day in the life of a family circus.
- B The story of the Wallenda family.
- C How to be a tightrope walker.

2 Read the text again and answer the questions.
1. What is different about Tino's walk along the street?
2. When did the Wallenda family start doing high-wire acts?
3. Why was 'The Great Pyramid' so dangerous?
4. How long has Tino been a member of the circus?
5. Why did he want to recreate 'The Great Pyramid'?
6. How did other members of his family react?

3 Find words and phrases in the text which match the definitions.

Paragraph A
1. slow walk for pleasure

Paragraph B
2. high point of an event

Paragraph C
3. fell down

Paragraph D
4. agreed with

Paragraph F
5. return the same way

4 Explain the meaning of the phrases.
1. death-defying acts (paragraph A)
2. to follow in his footsteps (paragraph F)

5 Discuss the questions.
1. Do you think that Tino was right to perform 'The Great Pyramid'? Why / Why not?
2. The Wallendas continued a 'family tradition' of being in a circus troupe. What do you think of Tino's decision to continue the family tradition?
3. Would you like to follow in your parents' footsteps?

Life on a high wire

A It was a windy day when Tino Wallenda went for a walk on the Strip – the most famous street in Las Vegas. But this was no ordinary stroll. Tino was on a thin steel wire over 30 metres up in the air, with no safety net! Tino is part of the Wallenda family, a circus troupe who have made history with their death-defying acts.

B The Wallendas have a strong family tradition. In the 1920s Tino's grandfather, Karl, started a high-wire troupe known as *The Flying Wallendas*. The troupe became part of the circus *The Greatest Show on Earth*, and the climax of their act was a seven-person pyramid. The pyramid was performed on a high wire without a net. It had three levels, with a woman at the top standing on a chair. It was an astonishing display of skill and courage.

C 'The Great Pyramid' was performed successfully by the Wallendas until 1962. Then disaster struck. The troupe were at the State Fair Coliseum in Detroit when the lead man slipped and the pyramid collapsed. A girl was in a chair at the top. As she fell, Karl Wallenda caught her and held onto her, but three men fell to the ground. Two of them were killed and the pyramid was never performed again – until recently.

D Tino joined the circus troupe when he was seventeen years old. Ever since then, he has wanted to perform 'The Great Pyramid'. Whenever people saw the Wallendas they only remembered the accident. Tino wanted to change this and complete the act successfully. However, not everyone in his family supported him – many felt it was too dangerous. But in March 1998, 'The Great Pyramid' was created once again, and in the same place – the State Fair Coliseum.

E Thousands of people looked on during the dangerous display. 'I've never seen anything like it in my life,' said one journalist. 'It's incredible.'

F Tino Wallenda is a brave man. After the show he spent a few moments thinking about his grandfather, Karl. Together they had proved to the world that a Wallenda never gives up and never turns back. 'He wanted me to follow in his footsteps,' he said, 'and I have.'

34 Unit 4

GRAMMAR

PRESENT PERFECT AND PAST SIMPLE

1 Read the sentences. Which are in the present perfect tense?

a Tino Wallenda **has worked** as a high-wire performer for many years.
b He **has already travelled** all over the world.
c He **performed** 'The Great Pyramid' five years ago.
d Tino **has just checked** the tight rope. You don't need to do it.

2 Answer the questions.

Which sentence describes:
1 a finished action in the past?
2 something which started in the past and continues in the present?
3 a recent past action which has a result in the present?
4 life experiences, where we don't refer to a specific time or period?

3 Choose the correct alternative.

1 Mark took up hang-gliding recently. He *has already had / already had* an accident!
2 Tino *has done / did* a lot of high-wire walks during his career.
3 Luke *has already started / started* abseiling three years ago.
4 *Have you been / Did you go to* the circus since it opened?
5 Rob *didn't go / hasn't been* skiing this year, yet.
6 After 'The Great Pyramid' accident, the Wallendas *looked into / have looked into* why it had happened.

> **NOTE!**
>
> *been* and *gone*
> She's been to the circus. = She went to the circus and came back.
> She's gone to the circus. = She went to the circus and she's still there.

4 Complete the text with the words below. Use the present perfect and the past simple.

> ~~work~~   come   contact   be   have   put   want
> throw   hurt

An unusual job

For the last ten years Chris Little *has worked* as a knife thrower at Smart's Circus, but recently he (1) _____ some problems. Why? Because he can't find an assistant! 'I (2) _____ an advertisement in the newspaper a month ago,' explained Chris, 'but since then only six people (3) _____ me.' Yesterday they all (4) _____ to the circus for an interview.

Everyone looked scared as Chris (5) _____ knives at them at 100 kph. 'I (6) _____ to be in a circus since I was a child,' said one candidate nervously, 'although I'd prefer to be a clown.'

But just how dangerous is it? 'I (7) _____ never _____ anyone,' insists Chris, although he did cut his last assistant once. At the time she (8) _____ his girlfriend, but not any more!

5 Imagine you are a journalist interviewing a candidate. Complete the questions. Use the past simple or the present perfect.

Why / you apply / for the job?
Why did you apply for the job?

1 How long / you want / to work in a circus?
2 you / always / dream / of being a knife thrower's assistant?
3 What job / you do before?
4 Why / you want / to change your job?
5 How / you feel / during your interview?
6 Chris / talk to you / afterwards?
7 Chris / offer you / the job yet?

6 Work in pairs. Take it in turns to interview each other. Imagine the candidate's answers.

Grammar reference page 99

Unit 4   35

Vocabulary

PREPOSITIONS OF MOVEMENT

1 Complete the sentences. Use the prepositions in the box.

| ~~into~~ | away from | round | out of | through |
| under | along | towards | | |

Jonathan is getting *into* the plane.

1 He's jumping _____ the plane.

2 Tino is walking _____ the tightrope.

3 He's walking _____ the hotel.

4 Belinda is going _____ the jungle.

5 She's walking _____ a lion.

6 Greg is swimming _____ the boat.

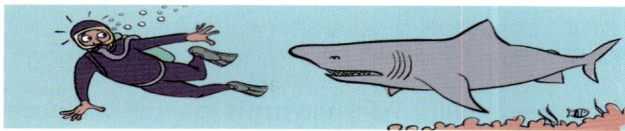

7 He's swimming _____ a shark.

Listening

2 Listen to the interview with 16-year-old Jonathan Cross. Which sport is he talking about?
1 football
2 bungee jumping
3 tennis
4 sky diving

3 Listen again. For questions 1–5, say whether the statements are true (T) or false (F).
1 Jonathan has done extreme sports before.
2 He was bored with school sports.
3 He felt calm before the jump.
4 Landing is the hardest part of the jump.
5 Jonathan never wants to jump again.

Pronunciation

4 Listen to the pronunciation of these sentences. Which words does the speaker stress?
1 How did you feel?
2 Weren't you afraid?

5 Listen and repeat the sentences. Mark the words which are stressed.
1 Have you ever done any dangerous sports before?
2 Why did you do it?
3 Can you tell me what happened next?
4 Did you experience any problems?

Speaking

6 Have you ever been in a dangerous or frightening situation? Where were you? Who were you with? Why was the situation dangerous or frightening?

7 Work in pairs. Ask questions about each other's experiences. Use the questions in the Pronunciation section and the prepositions of movement to help you.

Writing

LINKING WORDS: CONTRAST, REASON AND RESULT

1 Read the text and answer the questions.
1. How did the writer feel before and during the ride?
2. How do you think he felt after the ride?

> One of the most frightening rides I've ever experienced is called the Devil Dive. I was walking round a fair with some friends when I first saw the 100m dive. It looked quite dangerous, **so** we watched some people try it first to see what happened. It was strange because nobody screamed. I decided to have a go **because** I was curious.
>
> At first it was exciting **but** when I got to the top of the ride I felt sick with fear. The people on the ground below looked very small **and** my hands were shaking as I got into the seat. I really wanted to turn back. **However**, it was too late. Suddenly I was falling at 100kph – it was just like jumping out of a plane!
>
> Looking back on the experience, I've never been so terrified in my life. I **also** understand why devil divers never scream. They're far too frightened!

2 Complete the table. Use the linking words from the text.

LINKING WORDS	
Introducing a contrast	
Reason and result	so
Adding information	

3 Choose the correct alternative.
1. The dive looked frightening *but / so* I still did it.
2. Dave didn't go on the Devil Dive *however / because* he was feeling ill.
3. Rachel loves skiing *so / because* she booked a holiday in the Alps.
4. You need to be a good surfer *and / but* have a good sense of balance to windsurf.
5. Simon knows how to hang-glide. He can *also / however* sky dive.
6. Most extreme sports are dangerous. *So / However*, snowboarding is fairly safe.

4 Write an essay of 120–150 words about a dangerous or frightening situation that you have experienced. Use the plan to help you. Use linking words to connect your ideas, and prepositions of movement to describe what was happening.

> Paragraph 1: Say where you were and who was with you.
> Were you at school? At home? On holiday?
> Were you alone or with friends or your family?
>
> Paragraph 2: Describe what happened.
> Did someone have an accident?
> Why did it frighten you? What could have happened?
> How did you feel before / during / after the event?
>
> Paragraph 3: Describe what happened in the end.
> How did the people with you react?
> What happened in the end?

Unit 4

Units 3–4: revision

GRAMMAR

COMPARATIVES AND SUPERLATIVES

1 Complete the texts.

A 'Teenagers today have so much choice. The quality of education is (far / good) *far better*, and more young people are able to go to university. Travel is also (1 a lot / cheap) _____ so they can afford to visit places we never dreamed of visiting when we were young. And we didn't have things like mobile phones because technology was (2 much / expensive) _____ then. Life for young people is (3 much / easy) _____ now.'

B 'I think the worst thing is the pressure to do well. Teenagers today work (4 a lot / hard) _____ than teenagers ten years ago, so we have less free time. You could say we're (5 a bit / rich) _____, and it's true that we have more money, but things are (6 far / expensive) _____ now. Perhaps there are more things to do and our social life is (7 a little / exciting) _____, but we have to be (8 far / careful) _____. There's a lot more street crime nowadays.'

2 Rewrite the sentences. Use *as + as*, the comparatives or superlatives.

I've never played a computer game better than this one. (good)
This is *the best computer game I've ever played.*

1 There aren't any mobile phones that are smaller than this one. (small)
This is …
2 The CD cost less than I expected. (cheap)
The CD was …
3 Getting into university is more difficult than it used to be. (easy)
Getting into university isn't …
4 I haven't seen a film as scary as this one. (scary)
This is …
5 My sister isn't as young as me. (old)
My sister …
6 History and maths are equally difficult subjects. (hard)
History is …

QUANTIFIERS

3 Choose the correct alternative.

Today more and more students are using the Internet. Only (1) *a few / very little* students have their own computers, so (2) *much / most* teenagers use Internet cafés.

'I use a computer to send emails,' says 15-year-old Holly. 'So do (3) *all / much* of my friends.' What about homework? 'I do (4) *very few / a bit of* Internet research,' she says. 'Usually for school projects.'

(5) *Some / Any* students use the Internet more. 'I surf the web (6) *most / many* evenings,' says Simon, 16. 'But I also have (7) *a lot of / several* school work, so I don't have (8) *enough / plenty of* time to visit (9) *all / most* of my favourite sites.'

PRESENT PERFECT AND PAST SIMPLE

4 Rewrite the sentences. Use the present perfect simple.

I bought my MP3 player a year ago. (have / for)
I've had my MP3 player for a year.

1 Kate decided to be a circus performer when she was 11. (want / since)
2 My motorbike broke down last month. (not work / since)
3 Gina arrived in London two weeks ago. (be / for)
4 Paul met Holly a month ago. (know / for)
5 I bought a mobile phone when I was 13. (used / since)
6 I had lunch six hours ago. (not eat / for)

5 Complete the dialogue. Use the present perfect simple and past simple.

Helen (you / always / be) *Have you always been* interested in mountaineering?
Luke Yes, ever since I was 10 years old.
Helen (1 you / ever / climb) _____ Mount Everest?
Luke I (2 just / go on) _____ my third expedition there. I (3 already / climb) _____ to the top twice!
Helen That's impressive. What about the world's second highest mountain, K2?
Luke No, I (4 not climb / K2 / yet) _____.
Helen What's the most frightening thing (5 you / ever / experience) _____?
Luke Well, last year I (6 go) _____ to South Africa and I (7 do) _____ a sky dive. Unfortunately my parachute (8 not open) _____ so I (9 have) _____ to use an emergency parachute. Luckily it worked!

Revision 3–4

VOCABULARY

EDUCATION: VERB + NOUN

1 Choose the correct alternative.

I need to (1) *finish / make* my Maths homework before I start (2) *revising for / getting* the exam. It's tomorrow morning so there isn't much time. I should have started revising earlier, or at least (3) *studied / had* the subject more seriously in class. I need to (4) *pass / make* it, but I'll be lucky if I can (5) *answer / think* one question!

I wish I'd (6) *made / chosen* another subject, but it's really too late to (7) *have / drop* it now. I just have to (8) *take / make* the exam, I don't really (9) *do / have* a choice. It's the only way I'm going to (10) *get into / take* university.

PHRASAL VERBS

2 Complete the sentences. Use the phrasal verbs in the box.

look over   make up   look on   put up with
look up to   turn against   look back on
stick up for   look out for

Karl *looked over* his notes one last time before the exam.

1 When Ella _____ her time at school, she had a lot of good memories.
2 It didn't take long for us to _____ . It was a stupid argument anyway.
3 Neal always _____ his friends. He's a very loyal person.
4 Holly _____ her older brother. He was funny and very intelligent.
5 During the exam, the teacher _____ students who were trying to cheat.
6 Be careful! Gina will _____ you if you don't tell her the answers.
7 Rachel can be rude and unkind. I don't know why you _____ her.
8 The teacher _____ while we finished our projects, and she checked our work from time to time.

3 Complete the phrasal verbs.

When you climb a mountain, it's not just falling rocks that you need to (1) *l___ o___ f___*. It's also your climbing companions. Before you set out, you need to (2) *l___ i___* the background, character and climbing experience of your companions. Why? Because your life could depend on it!

There are no laws on a mountain, so it's not a good idea to (3) *f___ o___* with your companions. Climbing is a dangerous sport so you can't afford to be (4) *l___ d___* by your climbing partner. If someone (5) *t___ a___* you, things could get pretty scary. Your equipment is also vital. During an expedition you need to (6) *l___ a___* your equipment very carefully and make sure it all works. That way, climbing will be safe and enjoyable for you and your companions.

1 *look out for*   3 _____   4 _____
2 _____   5 _____   6 _____

ADVENTURE SPORTS

4 Match the sentences with the sports in the box.

abseiling   snowboarding   windsurfing
bungee jumping   sky-diving   hang-gliding

1 He's going quite fast down the slope now. _____
2 She's moving through the waves towards the beach. _____
3 He's jumping away from the bridge. _____
4 They're walking down the steep side of the mountain. _____
5 He doesn't want to jump out of the plane. _____
6 They're going to fly away from the hill, then land in a field. _____

PREPOSITIONS OF MOVEMENT

5 Complete the sentences with the words in the box.

along   through   round   towards (x2)   away from
into   out of   under

1 Karl was driving _____ the road when a cyclist in front of him fell off her bike. He stopped and got _____ his car to see if she was hurt.
2 'I'm not walking _____ the forest. It's getting dark.' 'Come on. It'll take far too long to walk _____ it.'
3 Jan hates mice. Whenever one runs _____ her, she panics and runs _____ it.
4 It was a beautiful evening, so we decided to go on a boat trip. After we had all got _____ the boat, we sailed down the river, _____ the bridge and _____ the sea.

> Now look at the song on page 95.

Revision 3–4   **39**

5 Living with danger

INTRODUCTION

1 Look at the pictures. What are the five disasters? What causes them?

1 *Disaster: drought*
   Causes: hot and dry weather, poor land management

READING

2 Read the text. What qualities do you need to be a 'Hotshot'?

3 Read the text again. For questions 1–6, choose the correct answer A, B or C.

1 Deborah's job is to
   A fly a helicopter.
   B rescue people.
   C save forests.

2 Hotshots stop fires with
   A water.
   B fire lines.
   C fire engines.

3 Most of the fires are started by
   A natural causes.
   B people.
   C windy weather.

4 If the fire is out of control
   A a helicopter can rescue the Hotshots.
   B the Hotshots use tents to protect themselves.
   C the Hotshots carry on firefighting.

5 Most Hotshots are
   A over 30 years old.
   B young women.
   C extremely fit and healthy.

6 Young people want to be Hotshots because of the
   A money they earn.
   B good exercise.
   C short working hours.

4 Find words in the text which match the definitions.

Paragraph A
1 bravery

Paragraph B
2 depending on (somebody)

Paragraph C
3 an increase in the temperature of the Earth's atmosphere
4 the effect of trapping gases in the Earth's atmosphere

Paragraph D
5 a large fire

Paragraph E
6 the best

DISCUSSION

5 Would you like to be a Hotshot? Why / Why not? Think about:
   • the working conditions
   • the money you could earn
   • the danger
   • the excitement
   • how you could help the environment

40   Unit 5

Hotshot firefighters

A At 6 a.m. Deborah Grant takes a helicopter to work. Equipped with an 18-kilo backpack, a first aid kit and a lot of courage, her task is to fight the worst forest fires America has ever seen. Deborah is part of 'Hotshots', an expert team of fire-fighters who risk their lives every day to stop forest fires from spreading.

B Hotshots climb up impossibly steep mountains where no fire engines can go. They can't carry water with them, so they stop the fires by cutting down trees. These are called 'fire lines' and Hotshots can work on them for up to 30 hours at a time. 'It's exhausting,' says 20-year-old Deborah, 'but you have to keep going. People are relying on us to protect them.'

D Tomorrow morning Deborah and the Hotshots are flying to Idaho to fight a blaze in the Payette National Forest. As usual the risks are high. 'You have to predict where the fire is going to go next,' explains Deborah. 'It can jump across large distances so you can easily get trapped.' As a last resort, when it's too dangerous for helicopters to pick them up, the Hotshots stay in fire-resistant 'tents' until the fire passes – often for as long as three hours.

C Experts say that an unusually hot summer caused by global warming and the greenhouse effect is responsible for the fires. Most of them start naturally, caused by lightning rather than cigarettes or camp fires. They are then spread by 40–60kph winds. So far this summer thousands of hectares of forest have been destroyed and hundreds of people have been evacuated.

E Yet despite the dangers, for many of these super-fit 20-year-olds being a highly-trained Hotshot is the ultimate summer job. They only work for three months but they earn a lot of money. 'I don't know where I'll be when I'm 30, but I definitely won't be here!' says Deborah, 'I'm just doing this for the summer. Then I'm going back to university.'

GRAMMAR

WILL, GOING TO AND THE PRESENT CONTINUOUS

1 Look at the examples and complete the rules. Use *will*, *going to* and *the present continuous*.

Next year global warming **will** increase.
'I can't carry this backpack.' 'I**'ll** carry it for you.'
The Hotshots **are flying** to Arizona tomorrow.
They**'re going to** fight a dangerous fire.
Look out! That tree **is going to** fall!

> 1 We use _____ for future plans or arrangements which often mention a time or place.
> 2 We use _____ for:
>   a a future intention or a plan when a decision has already been made.
>   b a prediction based on evidence now.
> 3 We use _____ for:
>   a decisions or offers that are made at the moment of speaking.
>   b general predictions.

2 Find six examples of *going to*, *will* and the present continuous in paragraphs D and E of the text on page 41. Match them with their uses in Exercise 1.

Tomorrow morning Deborah and the Hotshots are flying to Idaho ... Present continuous: use 1.

3 Choose the correct alternative.

1 'I've lost my map.'
   'I *'ll help / 'm going to help* you look for it.'
2 Deborah hasn't decided what to do next summer. Maybe she *'ll work / is working* in a bank.
3 The Hotshots are too close to the fire. Someone *is going to get / is getting* hurt.
4 Which fires *are the Hotshots fighting / will the Hotshots fight* in Idaho tomorrow morning?
5 Deborah has earned a lot of money. She *'s going to buy / 'll buy* a motorbike.
6 In the future, global warming *will cause / is causing* more forest fires.

4 Complete the interview. Use *will* or the present continuous.

Presenter	Deborah, what (do) *are you doing* tomorrow?
Deborah	Well, tomorrow morning I (1 go) _____ to Idaho to fight a fire. We (2 meet) _____ another team of Hotshots there.
Presenter	How are you going to get there?
Deborah	I (3 fly) _____ there in a helicopter.
Presenter	Do you think there (4 be) _____ a lot of fires this summer?
Deborah	I hope not, but the weather forecast says there'll be lots of dry weather.
Presenter	(5 you have) _____ time for a holiday this summer?
Deborah	No, I won't. I'll have to work most days until September.
Presenter	Do you think you (6 work) _____ as a Hotshot next year?
Deborah	Maybe!

5 Make sentences for the following situations. Use *will*, *going to* or the present continuous.

> This summer is going to be dry and hot. Make a general prediction.
>
> *There'll be lots of forest fires this summer.*

1 Your friend is making a camp fire. It's close to some trees. What do you say?
2 A friend asks you about your plans for this evening. You intend to watch a video. What do you say?
3 Your friend is sunbathing. He / She is starting to go red. What do you say?
4 Your friend invites you to the beach tomorrow, but it's the first day of your summer job. What do you say?
5 Your friend is having problems with her homework. You want to help. What do you say?

Grammar reference page 105

VOCABULARY

WORD BUILDING

1 We can form some nouns by adding *-tion*, *-ation*, or *-sion* to a verb. Sometimes the spelling also changes slightly. Complete the table.

VERB	NOUN
1 destroy	destruction
2 _____	pollution
3 product	_____
4 create	_____
5 _____	contribution
6 _____	information
7 decide	_____
8 determine	_____
9 _____	organization
10 imagine	_____

2 Complete the sentences with nouns from Exercise 1.

1 If we manage to control _____ from factories, we could reduce global warming.
2 You need courage and _____ to be a Hotshot. You also have to be very fit!
3 The _____ caused by the volcano was terrible. Thousands of people lost their homes.
4 Everyone made a small _____ to the environmental campaign.
5 People need more _____ about products they can recycle.
6 The continued _____ of greenhouse gases will seriously harm the environment.

3 Complete the newspaper article. Use the noun form of the verbs in the box.

> ~~discuss~~   predict   explode   solve   populate   civilize

Ever since the millennium, there has been a lot of *discussion* about how and when the world will end. Some people believe that a meteor will hit our planet, causing a huge (1) _____ that would destroy (2) _____. Other experts say that a dramatic increase in the world's (3) _____ means there won't be enough food to feed people, and some think that unless we find a (4) _____ to global warming, extreme weather will make life impossible. However the strangest (5) _____ is that tiny man-made robots will take over the world and destroy all other life forms!

4 Discuss the questions.

1 Can you name any environmental organizations?
2 Where can you find information about recycling in your area?
3 Which predictions in Exercise 3 do you think will happen?
4 What solutions to environmental pollution can you think of?

Unit 5   **43**

READING

1 Read the text. What is it about? Choose the correct alternative. Give reasons for your choice.
  A Another man-made disaster.
  B A disaster waiting to happen.
  C Volcanic island in danger.

2 Read the text again. Are the sentences true or false?
  1 A film company is making a disaster movie about Cumbre Vieja.
  2 Geologists say that they don't know when Cumbre Vieja will erupt.
  3 A tidal wave would take about four hours to cross the Atlantic.
  4 The tidal wave will get smaller as it crosses the Atlantic.
  5 People living in New York will be at risk.
  6 The tidal wave will travel in from the coast for eight hours.

3 Match the words from the text with the definitions.
  1 tidal wave   a people with special knowledge
  2 submerged   b a very large wave in the sea
  3 threat   c destroyed or seriously damaged
  4 experts   d enormous; extremely large
  5 vast   e under water
  6 devastated   f a possible danger in the future

4 Explain the meaning of the phrases from the text.
  1 If all goes according to plan (line 20)
  2 everything in its path (line 41)
  3 head for the hills (line 52)

CUMBRE VIEJA

A volcano suddenly erupts and a few minutes later a giant tidal wave is crossing the Atlantic at the speed of a jumbo jet. A few hours later this wall of water hits the east coast of the USA and every coastal city is completely submerged.

This is not just an idea for another disaster movie, it's a very real threat. The volcano is Cumbre Vieja on the island of La Palma in the Canaries, 450 kilometres off the north west coast of Africa. The danger is so real that geologists from all over the world have come together to investigate the volcano. Carl Pasco, one of the volcanologists who will be working on the project, says, 'We'll be studying Cumbre Vieja very closely for the next few years so that we'll be able to predict when the next eruption will be. If all goes according to plan, we believe that by the year 2010 we'll have discovered exactly how dangerous this volcano is.' However, Pasco and his team of experts are already warning that billions of tonnes of rock could fall into the sea from one side of Cumbre Vieja at any time, creating an enormous tidal wave 650 metres high. If this happens, the wave will then travel west for 6,000 kilometres across the Atlantic Ocean at about 800 kph. Fortunately, by the time it reaches the other side, seven and a half hours later, it will have decreased in size and it will be 'only' 50 metres high. However, it will still be powerful enough to travel for 20 kilometres inland from the coast, destroying buildings, trees, bridges, everything in its path. By this time, vast cities like New York will have been devastated. People living on the coast will have less than eight hours to escape to safety after warnings have been broadcast. People living in low-lying states like Florida will be affected even more severely.

Cumbre Vieja last erupted in 1949 and similar volcanoes have erupted every few decades. So a disaster could happen at any time. And if it does, the entire population of the east coast of the USA will need to head for the hills – before it's too late.

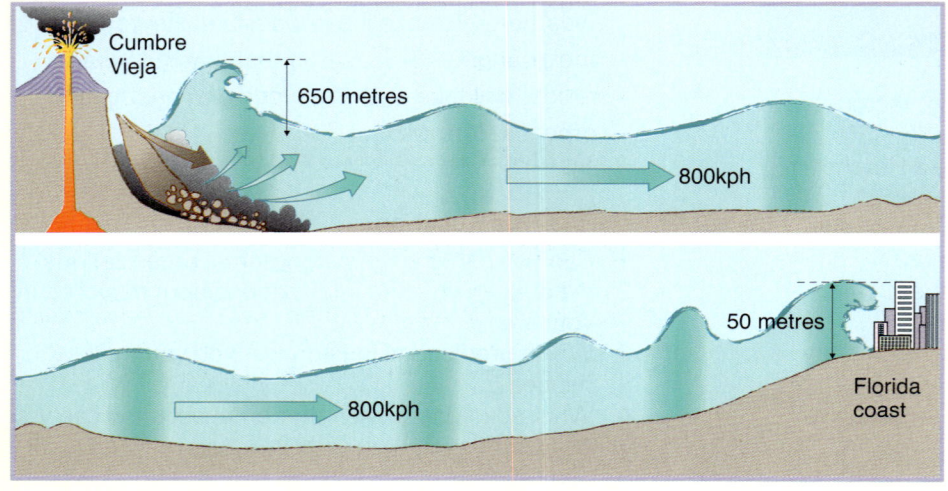

44 Unit 5

GRAMMAR

FUTURE CONTINUOUS

1 Read the sentence and complete the rule. Use *will* and *be*.

We **will be studying** the volcano for the next few years.

> We use _____ + _____ + verb + *-ing* to talk about something in progress at a certain time in the future.

2 Complete the table.

FUTURE CONTINUOUS			
Affirmative	Negative	Question	Short answer
We will be studying.	_____ studying.	_____ studying.	Yes, _____. No, _____.

3 Complete the sentences. Use the future continuous.

For the next few years a group of geologists (live) *will be living* on La Palma.
1 They (work) _____ hard.
2 They (not have) _____ many holidays.
3 Where they (stay) _____?
4 They (stay) _____ in the capital, Santa Cruz.
5 The volcanologists (use) _____ a lot of scientific instruments.
6 They (send) _____ their reports to New York.

4 Work in pairs. Ask and answer questions about what you will be doing in the future.

'What will you be doing at nine o'clock this evening?'
'I'll probably be watching TV or listening to music.'

- at nine o'clock this evening
- next Saturday evening
- next summer
- in a years' time
- in five years' time

FUTURE PERFECT

5 Read the sentence and complete the rule. Use *will* and *have*.

By 2010 we**'ll have discovered** how dangerous this volcano is.

> We use _____ + _____ + past participle to talk about something that will be completed before a certain time in the future.

6 Complete the table.

FUTURE PERFECT			
Affirmative	Negative	Question	Short Answer
It will have finished.	It _____.	_____ finished?	Yes, _____. / No, _____.

7 Complete these sentences about the year 2010 with verbs in the future perfect.

I (leave) home
I'll have left home.
1 I (finish) _____ university.
2 I (learn) _____ to speak much better English.
3 I (get) _____ a job.
4 But I (not leave) _____ this city.
5 I (buy) _____ my own apartment near here.

8 Complete the TV interview with a volcanologist. Use the future perfect.

> ~~leave~~   start   finish   say   find   meet   find out   fly   not finish

Presenter So Karen, this time next week you*'ll have left* London.
Karen That's right, I (1) _____ goodbye to all my friends in London and I (2) _____ out to the island where Cumbre Vieja is.
Presenter Have you got somewhere to stay?
Karen No, not yet but I hope I (3) _____ somewhere to stay by the end of the first week.
Presenter (4) _____ you _____ work by then?
Karen No, probably not, but I (5) _____ the people I'm going to be working with.
Presenter You're going to be there for some time. When (6) _____ you _____ your work?
Karen We (7) _____ it until about 2010.
Presenter And what (8) _____ you _____ by that time?
Karen Hopefully by then we'll be able to predict when Cumbre Vieja is going to erupt.
Presenter I'm glad to hear that Karen. Thank you.

Grammar reference page 105

Unit 5   45

VOCABULARY

WEATHER

1 Look at the words in the box and complete the list of weather types.

> blizzard   breeze   downpour   drizzle   gale
> haze   hurricane   mist   shower   sleet

1 wind _____
2 fog   _____
3 rain _____
4 snow _____

2 Look at your lists from Exercise 1 again. Put the words in order with the 'weakest' first.

3 Are the sentences true or false? Correct the false sentences.
1 A gale is a stronger wind than a hurricane.
2 A shower doesn't last long.
3 If there's a breeze it's dangerous to go outside.
4 You can see further in fog than in mist.
5 It's dangerous to drive in a blizzard.
6 Drizzle is a very light type of rain. It often lasts all day.

4 Look at the weather map. Complete the weather forecast with words from Exercise 1.

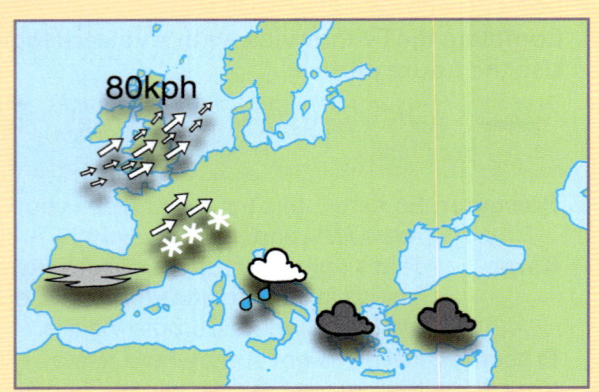

Good evening. Well, in Europe tomorrow we're going to have a lot of bad weather. I'll start in central France, where the temperatures are going to be very low with strong winds and snow. (1) _____ will make driving conditions there extremely dangerous. The north coast of Spain will have dense (2) _____, with visibility down to 20m. In London we're expecting (3) _____, with wind speeds of over 80 kilometres an hour. In Italy it won't be cold, but take your umbrella because we're expecting occasional short (4) _____ . In Greece and Turkey the rain will be lighter but there will be a constant (5) _____ .

5 Describe the weather in your area in January, April, July and November. Use words from Exercise 1.

LISTENING

6 Listen to the weather report and answer the questions.
1 What is the reporter worried about?
2 Which part of America is affected?

7 Listen again. For questions 1–6, complete the notes.

Name of reporter:	1
Name of hurricane:	2
Present position of hurricane:	3
Maximum wind speed:	4
Damage expected:	5
Time when emergency will end:	6

SPEAKING

8 Work in pairs. Student A is a newscaster in London, student B is a reporter in a country where a natural disaster is happening. Prepare a similar news report.

Student A
- Introduce the reporter
- Explain where the report is coming from

Ask questions about:
- the type of disaster (for example a hurricane, a tidal wave, or a flood)
- what is happening now
- what is going to happen soon
- the damage expected
- why it is dangerous

Student B
Answer Student A's questions with information about the disaster.

9 Act out your news report.

46   Unit 5

Writing

Relevant information

1 You are going to read a factual essay about global warming. Which of the statements about the topic is irrelevant?

a The earth's temperature has risen by almost one degree over the last 100 years.
b When it's hot, people like to swim in the sea.
c The greenhouse effect causes global warming.

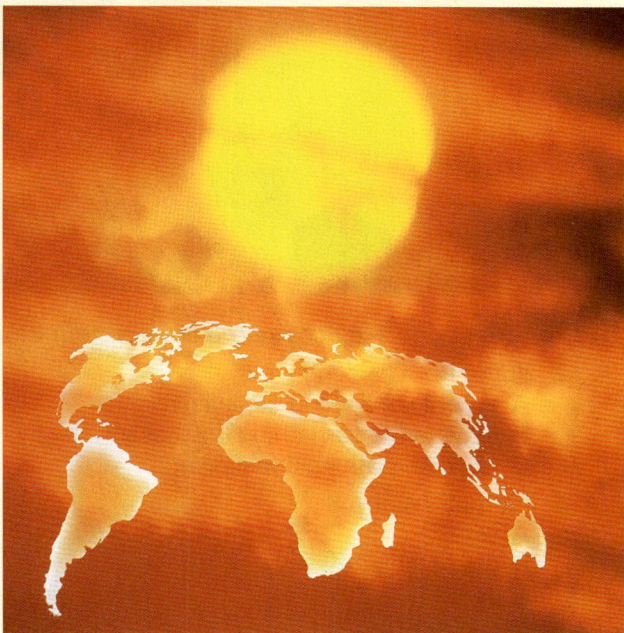

2 Read the essay. Which three sentences contain irrelevant information?

> <u>The earth is getting hotter</u>
>
> It is a fact that the average temperature of the earth is going up. The greenhouse effect means that the sun's heat is trapped, and so we get global warming. As a result, summers are getting hotter and drier. Yesterday I felt really hot – the temperature here reached 38 degrees!
>
> Having drier summers creates problems. In many countries it is causing huge forest fires. These fires cause a lot of damage. In my opinion, dry summers are fine if you can spend all summer lying on the beach. However, there are also more droughts because the earth is getting hotter. This makes it difficult to grow food in some areas. When I'm hot I don't feel like eating much, though.
>
> To sum up, global warming is creating lots of environmental problems. It is changing the earth's weather, and it is leading to a number of disasters.

3 Read the following notes for a factual essay about extreme weather. Which notes should not be included in the essay?

> 1 The effects of extreme weather are becoming more serious.
> 2 Extreme weather is mainly caused by global warming.
> 3 I don't think we're doing enough to prevent global warming.
> 4 Extreme weather damages buildings and the food we grow. It can be very dangerous.
> 5 Extreme weather includes things like hurricanes, floods and droughts.
> 6 There were severe storms in this area last winter.
> 7 Floods are becoming more and more common.
> 8 Scientists predict that by the year 2100 the earth's temperature will have risen five degrees and we will have more extreme weather.
> 9 We can reduce the amount of damage caused by extreme weather by controlling global warming.
> 10 I don't mind if the earth gets a few degrees warmer.

4 You are going to write an essay about extreme weather. First look at the title and plan your essay.

'In the future, extreme weather will cause many more disasters.'

1 Brainstorm your own ideas and add them to the ideas from Exercise 3.
2 Cross out any ideas which are irrelevant.

5 Write an essay of 120–150 words. Use the paragraph plan below to help you.

> Paragraph 1: Introduction: what is extreme weather?
> How is it linked to global warming?
>
> Paragraph 2: What disasters are caused by extreme weather?
> What damage do these disasters do?
>
> Paragraph 3: Conclusion

6 Fears and phobias

INTRODUCTION

1 Look at the pictures. How frightening do you think these things are? Why? Put them in order.

READING

2 Read the text. Which of the things in the pictures are mentioned?

3 Read the text again and answer the questions.
   1 What is unusual about Guy Allen?
   2 What is the difference between fear and a phobia?
   3 What are three effects that phobias can have on people?
   4 What can people develop phobias about?
   5 Why might a child develop a phobia?
   6 Why are some people frightened of swimming in the sea?
   7 How do our basic instincts affect the way we behave?
   8 Why aren't people scared of buses?

4 Find the words in the text. Answer the questions for each word.

   | suffer from | harmless | unbearable | tremble |
   | ancestors | run over | | |

   1 Is it positive or negative?
   2 Does it have a negative prefix (for example *in*-)?
   3 Does it have a suffix (for example -*ful*)?
   4 Do you recognise part of the word (for example 'instinct' in 'instinctively')?

5 For questions 1–6 choose the correct definition.
   1 suffer from (line 12)
      A accept something unpleasant
      B experience something unpleasant
      C avoid something unpleasant
   2 harmless (line 14)
      A safe
      B predictable
      C awful
   3 unbearable (line 17)
      A very enjoyable
      B too easy
      C too terrible to accept
   4 tremble (line 19)
      A short, quick movements
      B slow, calm movements
      C short, careful movements
   5 ancestors (line 48)
      A people who are living now
      B people who lived a long time before you
      C people who will live after you
   6 run over (line 49)
      A followed something
      B driven over by something
      C frightened by something

DISCUSSION

6 Discuss the questions.
   1 What is the most frightening film you've ever seen? Why was it frightening? Did you develop a phobia because of it?
   2 What types of phobia are mentioned in the text? What other phobias have you heard of? What things are you afraid of?

48 Unit 6

What are you scared of?

Guy Allen is a film stuntman with years of experience. He's jumped out of planes, driven cars into rivers and climbed the highest buildings with no ropes. If you ask him to act in a dangerous scene, he'll do it. But if he sees a spider he'll be terrified! Guy is one of many people who suffer from phobias, or a fear of things that are usually harmless.

Most of us are scared of something, but people with severe phobias find day-to-day life unbearable. They often have panic attacks and find it hard to breathe. They become nervous, they sweat and their hands tremble; some people pass out, others are frozen to the spot. These violent attacks can be caused by spiders, snakes, or even birds. But it's not just animals that provoke fear – some phobias are caused by the weather. In fact people can suffer from everything from a fear of heights to fear of thunder!

Nearly 8% of all adults have a phobia of one sort or another. But why do we have them? One explanation is that they are caused by other people. When a child sees its mother scream at a mouse, for example, they associate it with danger. Another explanation could be a traumatic childhood experience, such as an attack by a dog. Some people even develop phobias after reading a book or watching a film. The film *Jaws* was about a man-eating shark. When it was first seen by cinema-goers they were terrified by it. Today, over twenty years later, some people are still too afraid to go into the sea!

A final explanation could be our basic instincts. Primitive humans instinctively avoided dangerous animals such as snakes and poisonous spiders. If you were afraid, you were more likely to survive. Nowadays buses are far more dangerous than spiders, but people like Guy Allen are more frightened of spiders. Perhaps it's because our ancestors were never run over by buses!

GRAMMAR

PASSIVE: PRESENT AND PAST

1 Read the sentences. Which are active and which are passive?
   a   The weather **causes** some phobias.
   b   Some phobias **are caused** by the weather.
   c   The film **was seen** in 1975.
   d   Cinema-goers **saw** the film in 1975.

2 Choose the correct alternative.

> 1 In *active / passive* sentences we know who or what does the action.
> 2 In *active / passive* sentences we often don't know who does the action, or who or what does the action isn't important.
> 3 In *active / passive* sentences we can use *by* + noun to say who or what does the action.

3 Complete the second sentence so that it has a similar meaning to the first sentence.
   People's fears are studied by psychologists.
   Psychologists study people's fears.
   1 Some phobias are caused by violent films.
     Violent films _____ phobias.
   2 The film *Jaws* was seen by lots of people.
     Lots of people _____ *Jaws*.
   3 The book was bought by millions of people.
     Millions of people _____ book .
   4 Was anyone attacked by a shark?
     Did _____ anyone.
   5 People with phobias are helped by psychologists.
     Psychologists _____ phobias.

4 Rewrite the sentences in the passive.

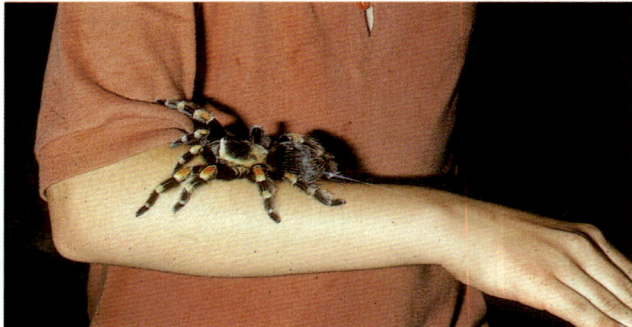

   Phobias affect 8% of adults.
   8% of adults are affected by phobias.
   1 Scientists conducted an experiment on Guy Allen.
   2 First they asked him a lot of questions.
   3 Then they showed him a spider.
   4 After that they noted his reaction to the spider.
   5 The spider didn't harm Guy.
   6 Spiders rarely attack people.
   7 Some people keep spiders as pets.

5 Complete the text. Use the passive or active of the verbs below.

> ~~attack~~ attack see swim kill think hit
> fall survive call

Boat attacked by shark

Yesterday a fishing boat *was attacked* by a hungry, six-metre shark off the coast of Sydney in Australia. Five fishermen (1) _____ the terrifying attack, although two men nearly (2) _____ into the sea.

Several hours later, the same shark (3) _____ near the beach, and a boat full of tourists (4) _____ for over half an hour. 'The boat (5) _____ a few times,' said tourist Brad Hunter, 'then the shark (6) _____ to the surface and looked at us. It was huge!' The coastguards (7) _____, but by the time they arrived, the shark had disappeared.

There are many shark attacks in Australia and each year one or two people (8) _____. Attacks often happen because sharks (9) _____ that people are fish.

6 Rewrite the newspaper headlines. Use the passive and add the missing words.

   Woman saved by dog
   A woman was saved by a dog.
   1 School destroyed by earthquake
   2 Burglars arrested in art gallery
   3 Runaway car stopped by 5-year-old
   4 UFOs spotted in China

7 Discuss what you think each story is about. Think about where it happened, who was involved, and what happened in the end.

Grammar reference page 106

Vocabulary

CONFUSING WORDS

1 Complete the sentences. Choose the correct alternative.

1 **bring / take**
   a Could you _____ my bag for me? I've got too much to carry.
   b Could you _____ me my coat? It's getting cold.
2 **control / check**
   a People with phobias find it difficult to _____ their fear.
   b You should _____ what time your train leaves. You don't want to be late.
3 **rare / strange**
   a The King Cobra snake is very _____ . There are only a few thousand in the world.
   b It's _____ that people are scared of spiders. They're harmless!
4 **nervous / angry**
   a Guy felt _____ when he saw the spider move.
   b There's no need to get _____ . It was an accident!
5 **sensible / sensitive**
   a Simon is _____ and reasonable. I'm sure he'll solve the problem.
   b Julie's very _____ . She often gets upset about things.
6 **announcement / advertisement**
   a Paul saw an _____ in the newspaper for a job as a stuntman.
   b Tina's _____ about her decision to study spiders surprised everyone.
7 **notice / news**
   a The _____ on all the channels was about the shark attack.
   b He put up a _____ about the phobia disussion group in the supermarket.

2 Complete the text. Choose the correct alternative.

Jade Faraday is a (sensible) / sensitive person, but she used to be terrified of spiders! However, recently she cured her phobia.

'Last summer I saw an (1) announcement / advertisement for a holiday on a tropical island. It was a beautiful island, with beach chalets next to the sea, so I decided to go!

I arrived late at night, and the first thing I did was (2) check / control the beach chalet for spiders. At first I couldn't see anything because the light didn't work! Fortunately I'd (3) brought / taken a torch. I switched it on and there were spiders everywhere! At first I was (4) nervous / angry and that first night I couldn't sleep. When I got up the next day, I realised I couldn't stop them getting into the chalet. It may sound (5) strange / rare, but I decided to take pictures of them. I thought it would help me to get used to them. Amazingly it worked, and after two weeks I was able to touch one. My family were very surprised by the (6) news / notice when they heard.

Today spiders don't scare me at all. In fact I'm very interested in (7) rare / strange species and I often take their photograph!'

Unit 6

READING

1 Read the text and match the topics (1–5) with the paragraphs (A–E).
1 The origins of the superstition.
2 Examples of unfortunate things that have happened.
3 Are you afraid of the number 13?
4 Living without the number 13.
5 Someone who is not superstitious.

2 Find evidence in the text to support the sentences.
1 Nowadays people still worry about the number 13.
2 Fear of the number 13 began a long time ago.
3 People in some countries believe that certain days of the week bring bad luck.
4 Strange things have happened on the 13th day of the month.
5 Nick Matsoukas isn't superstitious.
6 The number 13 isn't always unlucky.

3 Find the words in the text. For numbers 1–6, choose the correct definition.
1 skyscrapers (line 12)
  A small buildings
  B old buildings
  C tall buildings
2 uneasy about (line 22)
  A nervous about
  B relaxed about
  C angry about
3 justify (line 31)
  A excuse
  B support
  C disprove
4 launched (line 35)
  A put something into the sea
  B take something out of the sea
  C rescue something from the sea
5 doomed (line 37)
  A very successful
  B certain to fail
  C fortunate
6 founded (line 50)
  A suggested
  B closed down
  C started

What's in a number?

A How superstitious are you? Would you live in a flat on the 13th floor? Would you fly on the 13th of the month? If the answer is no, then you suffer from triskaidekaphobia – or fear of the number 13.

B People all over the world are frightened of the number 13. For instance, in America many skyscrapers have been built with no 13th floor. In France many streets have been planned with no 13th house. In Italy the lottery has no number 13; and if you've been given a name with 13 letters, people say you'll have bad luck. But why?

C Ever since Roman times we've been uneasy about the number 13. The Romans believed that demons met in groups of 13 and the 13th member was the Devil. In Chinese mythology, writers said that there were 13 obstacles in the way of good fortune. In fact in many countries the number 13 is extremely unlucky when it falls on a Friday or a Tuesday. In ancient Rome Friday was the day when criminals were killed, and Tuesday was associated with Mars, the god of war.

D But is there any evidence to justify these fears? Apparently, yes. In 1796 a British Royal Navy ship called 'HMS Friday' went on its first voyage on Friday 13th. The ship was never seen or heard of again. Since then the Navy has launched ships on every day of the week except a Friday! Another famous disaster happened in 1970 when the doomed NASA rocket, Apollo 13 took off at 13.13. The mission nearly killed all the astronauts on board. It was cancelled on 13th April.

E However if your name has 13 letters don't despair. Nick Matsoukas was born on June 13th and is the thirteenth child in his family, but he has never been afraid of the bad-luck stories and he has never had his fortune told. In fact he founded a 'National Committee of Thirteen Against Superstition, Prejudice, and Fear' – on Friday 13th. And he survived!

52   Unit 6

GRAMMAR

PASSIVE: PRESENT PERFECT

1 Look at the example. How do we form the present perfect passive?

You've **been given** a name with 13 letters.

2 Find two more examples of present perfect passive sentences in paragraph B of the text on page 52.

3 Rewrite the sentences. Use the present perfect passive.

> People have considered the number 13 unlucky for many years.
> *The number 13 has been considered unlucky for many years.*

1 People have recorded strange events on Friday 13th.
2 Nick Matsoukas has started a society against superstition.
3 People have written books about superstitions.
4 Psychologists have studied our fear of 13.
5 Ghosts have haunted the old house for years.
6 People have seen strange things.

4 Look at the pictures. Write sentences with the present perfect passive using the prompts below.

> door / unlock   mirror / break   window / open
> the jewels / steal   ~~house / burgle~~

The house has been burgled.

1 _____   2 _____

3  _____   4 _____

5 Complete the sentences. Use the present perfect active or passive.

1 Many films (make) _____ about Friday 13th.
2 Statistics show that more accidents (happen) _____ on Friday 13th.
3 Mexicans (always / believe) _____ that the number 13 is lucky.
4 Lots of books (write) _____ about superstitions.
5 People (fascinate) _____ by the supernatural for centuries.
6 Horoscopes (read) _____ by people all over the world for a long time.
7 In some countries people (decide) _____ not to travel on Friday 13th.
8 A lot of my friends (frighten) _____ by horror films.

HAVE / GET SOMETHING DONE

6 Read the sentences and choose the correct rule.

Brent's motorbike is very old. He's taken it to the garage to **have** it **repaired**.

Dani wants to **get** her new mobile **connected**.

> We can use *have / get something done* to talk about things which are:
> a done by ourselves.
> b done by other people.

7 Complete the sentences. Use *have / get something done* and the words in brackets.

> Nick Matsoukas isn't superstitious. He (never / fortune / tell).
> *He's never had his fortune told.*

1 Patrick looks different. I think he (hair / cut) _____.
2 We can't surf the Internet. I (not / computer / fix) _____.
3 I (holiday photos / develop) _____. Do you want to see them?
4 Emma walked to school. She (not / her bike / repair) _____.
5 My parents (cable TV / install) _____. We often watch the movie channel.
6 The car sounds odd. You'd better (engine / check) _____.

8 Discuss the questions.

1 Have you ever had your fortune told? Would you like to have it told? Why / Why not?
2 When was the last time your TV / radio / Walkman broke down? Did you get it repaired by someone? Who?
3 How often do you have your hair cut? Where do you get it cut?

Grammar reference page 106

Unit 6   53

VOCABULARY

ADJECTIVE + PREPOSITION

1 Read the sentences. What prepositions come after the adjectives?
  a Mark was **excited about** the haunted house.
  b Kate is **scared of** the dark.
  c Dan is **keen on** horoscopes.

2 Complete the table. Use the prepositions in the box.

| ~~on~~ | of | to | with | by | about | from |

	ADJECTIVE	PREPOSITION
1	keen	on
2	scared, tired	____
3	excited, nervous	____
4	popular, fed up	____
5	fascinated, surprised	____
6	similar, kind	____
7	different	____

3 Complete the sentences about yourself.

I'm very keen on programmes about nature.

1 I'm very keen …
2 I used to be scared …
3 I never get tired …
4 I'm often surprised …
5 I'm fascinated …
6 I sometimes get fed up …
7 I'm quite similar …

LISTENING

4 Listen to the first part of the story. Answer the questions.

1 Where were they driving?
2 How did Ray feel?
3 What did they see?
4 What do you think happened next?

5 Listen to the second part of the story. Complete the sentences.

1 It was too late for Ray to …
2 When they hit the truck, the cars …
3 When Ray and Brett got to the road …
4 Ray couldn't explain …

PRONUNCIATION

6 Listen to how the weak forms of *was* and *were* are pronounced in the sentences.

1 It was a warm evening.
2 They were racing towards us.

7 Listen and repeat the sentences.

1 He was very tired.
2 We were really panicking.
3 What were they doing?
4 It was too late!
5 There was nothing there.

SPEAKING

8 What do you think is the explanation for the strange encounter above? Work in pairs. Discuss the options (1–4) and decide which is the most probable.

1 a dream   3 the supernatural
2 a hallucination 4 aliens

A *Ray says he was very tired. Perhaps he fell asleep and had a dream.*
B *Maybe, but I think …*

9 Have you ever had a strange dream? Describe what happened.

1 Where were you?
2 Who was in your dream?
3 How did you feel?

54 Unit 6

WRITING

PARAGRAPHING

1 Read the two essays. Are the writers for or against horoscopes?

'Horoscopes are a waste of time.' What do you think?

1

Today almost every newspaper and magazine has a horoscope. Although it's true that people enjoy reading them, I think that they're a waste of time. I think the worst thing about horoscopes is the fact that they make people superstitious. I also think they make people believe that things can happen without them doing anything. I also think that the predictions are so general that they could mean anything. If there was nothing else to read, I still wouldn't read my horoscope. I'm tired of them!

In short, I think that they are a waste of time. Why read horoscopes when you could do something else more interesting?

2

A Horoscopes have always been popular with millions of people. Every day people read them in newspapers and magazines, but are they a waste of time? I'd say they're not.

B There are many reasons why people enjoy horoscopes. Firstly, most people love to read about themselves. Secondly, it's fun to read about things you might do or how you might feel that day or that week. Thirdly, it's exciting when predictions come true.

C However, horoscopes can be disappointing. They might say the same thing too often, and sometimes nothing happens.

D In conclusion I believe that horoscopes aren't a waste of time. In my opinion, they're very entertaining. I always get excited about reading mine!

2 Read the essays again and answer the questions.
Which essay:
1 is organized into logical paragraphs?
2 uses different expressions to introduce an opinion?
3 uses expressions to order ideas?
4 do you think is best?

NOTE!

Paragraphing
After brainstorming ideas and crossing out irrelevant points, it's a good idea to organize your ideas into paragraphs. Think about points that you are going to include in the introduction, the main part of your essay and the conclusion.

3 Match the paragraph topics (1–4) with paragraphs A–D in essay 2.
1 Summarizing your opinion. _____
2 Arguments against horoscopes. _____
3 Introducing the essay topic and your opinion. _____
4 Arguments for horoscopes. _____

4 Write a for and against essay of about 100–120 words on the following question. Use the ideas and the paragraph plan to help you.
What are the arguments for and against having your fortune told?

> It's great fun, but you shouldn't take it seriously.

> People might be disturbed by the experience.

> Fortune tellers take advantage of people.

> I'd be fascinated by the predictions, but what if they were bad?

> It's impossible to predict the future.

Paragraph 1: Introduction.
Paragraph 2: Arguments against having your fortune told.
Paragraph 3: Arguments for having your fortune told.
Paragraph 4: Conclusion – state your opinion.

Unit 6

Units 5–6: revision

GRAMMAR

THE FUTURE

1 Choose the correct alternative.

> 28-year-old Hannah Grey is anxious. She's got a plane ticket and she (1) *'s going to fly / will fly* for the first time today. At the moment she's sitting in a room in an airport with 20 other nervous people. They all have their tickets, and in two hours' time they (2) *'re getting on / 'll get on* a plane to Manchester. However, this isn't any ordinary flight. This flight is part of a course for people who are scared of flying.
>
> 'Before we leave we (3) *'ll have / 're having* a lecture about safety and how the plane works,' says Hannah. 'Hopefully that (4) *'ll help / 's helping* everyone to relax. Then, we're boarding the plane and flying from London to Manchester,' she adds. 'We (5) *'ll only be / 're only being* in the air for 30 minutes but I'm not looking forward to it. However, I joined the course so that I could get over my fear, and so I (6) *'ll do / 'm going to do* it.
>
> The last time Hannah booked a flight she was so nervous that she couldn't get on the plane. 'I hope I (7) *'ll feel / 'm feeling* calmer during the flight', she says, smiling nervously. 'I need to get used to flying because I (8) *'m visiting / 'll visit* my sister in Florida this summer, and I've already booked my ticket.'

2 Look at the activities Hannah will / won't have done by the end of her holiday in Florida. Make sentences with the verbs and the future perfect.

> 1 visit Disneyworld ✓
> 2 see the dolphins at Seaworld ✗
> 3 swim in the sea ✓
> 4 watch a drive-in movie ✗
> 5 buy some souvenirs in a shopping mall ✓
> 6 eat some Florida seafood ✓

1 *She'll have been to Disneyworld.*
2
3
4
5
6

PASSIVE

3 Complete the text. Use the passive (past, present or present perfect) form of the verbs.

> Forest fires (1 cause) _____ by many different things. Sometimes camp fires (2 not put out) _____ properly, and other times trees (3 hit) _____ by lightning. But the most dangerous forest fires (4 usually / start) _____ by lightning in dry summers. These fires (5 often / spread) _____ by high winds and the flames are usually over ten metres high. Hotshots (6 send) _____ to deal with these fires and special equipment (7 use) _____ to fight them.
>
> Over the last few years there have been huge forest fires all over the world. Last summer over 258,000 hectares of forest (8 destroy) _____ in America, and hundreds of houses (9 burn down) _____. Luckily only a few people (10 injure) _____.
>
> Forest fires (11 study) _____ by scientists for a long time, and recently a new way of controlling them (12 develop) _____. During dry summers, there are clouds but there isn't any rain, so scientists use a special chemical to produce rain. The chemical (13 drop) _____ onto a cloud and rain falls on the dry forest below. In the future, forest fires may be a thing of the past.

HAVE / GET SOMETHING DONE

4 Complete the sentences. Use *have / get something done* and the words in brackets.

> This week Richard (his car / mend) *is having his car mended,* so he's travelling to work by bus.

1 Donna (a photo / take) _____ of herself in Hollywood.
2 Helen (her hair / cut) _____ while she was on holiday.
3 We (our DVD player / repair) _____ at the moment, so let's watch TV instead.
4 Jamie looks different. He (his hair / dye) _____ green!
5 I'm bored with my bedroom. I want to (it / redecorate) _____ .
6 'Let's get Kate something nice for her birthday.' 'Good idea. We could (flowers / deliver) _____ to her house.'

VOCABULARY

WORD BUILDING

1 Complete the sentences. Use the noun form of the words in the box.

> ~~discuss~~   determine   civilize   organize   solve
> populate   pollute

We had an interesting *discussion* about the environment.
1 Last year the world's _____ was over 6 billion.
2 If we don't look after our natural resources, human _____ may not survive.
3 Many environmental _____ advertize in newspapers and magazines.
4 Scientists are trying to find a _____ to global warming.
5 The river _____ was so bad that all the fish died.
6 The environmental group showed great _____ to publicise the clean river campaign.

WEATHER

2 Complete the text. Choose the correct alternative A, B or C.

> I've lived on the west coast of Scotland all my life. During the summer it's a beautiful place to be. Early in the morning there is a light (1) ___ on the sea and a warm (2) ___ blows in from the south. But winter is completely different. When the bad weather arrives, there are usually strong (3) ___. It's extremely cold and there is often ice and (4) ___ on the beach. In fact once we had a (5) ___ that lasted two weeks!

1 A downpour   B mist   C sleet
2 A gale   B drizzle   C breeze
3 A showers   B breezes   C gales
4 A snow   B floods   C haze
5 A wind   B blizzard   C shower

3 Complete the sentences. Use the words in the box.

> hurricane   fog   wind   flood   sleet   downpour

1 The _____ was so thick we couldn't see where we were going.
2 It was a typical winter's day. It was wet and extremely cold, and the rain had become _____.
3 Everyone got soaked by the sudden _____. It was completely unexpected.
4 We can't go sailing; there's no _____ today.
5 After weeks of rain, the river overflowed. The _____ damaged hundreds of homes.
6 The _____ came in from the sea. It destroyed everything in its path.

CONFUSING WORDS

4 Choose the correct alternative.

Ever since I was a child I've been (1) *nervous / angry* about storms. Most children have (2) *sensitive / sensible* feelings about thunder and lightning, but unfortunately I never grew out of it. I know it sounds (3) *rare / strange*, but I just can't (4) *check / control* it. I always (5) *take / bring* an umbrella with me wherever I go, and before I go out I always (6) *control / check* the weather forecast to see if there's going to be a storm. If there is, I stay indoors.

Then two weeks ago I saw an (7) *announcement / advertisement* in the newspaper. It was for a class about phobias for people like me. In fact the first class is tomorrow and I just might go – if it isn't raining …

ADJECTIVES + PREPOSITION

5 Complete the questions with a preposition.
1 Are you scared _____ heights?
2 What type of things do you get excited _____?
3 Which sports are you keen _____?
4 How are you different _____ your parents?
5 Are you fascinated _____ new technology?
6 In what ways are you similar _____ your best friend?

> Now look at the song on page 96.

Revision 5–6   **57**

7 Inventions

INTRODUCTION

1 Match the inventions in the box to the pictures.

> matches   fridge   mobile telephone   aeroplane
> personal stereo   pencil

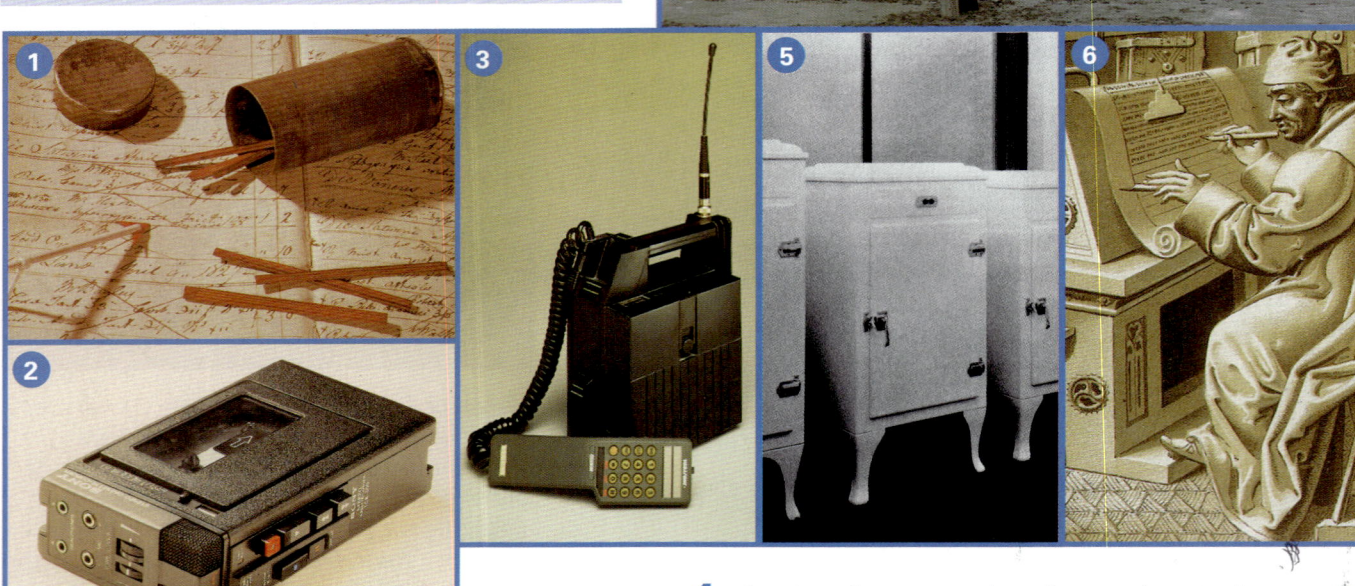

2 Which of the inventions in Exercise 1 do you think is the most important? Why? Which do you think is the least important?

I think matches are really important because without them we wouldn't be able to light a fire as easily.

READING

3 Read the text and answer the questions.
1. In what ways is SoloTrek like a helicopter?
2. Why could a SoloTrek be very useful?
3. Where are SoloTrek's inventors working?
4. What makes SoloTrek safe to fly?
5. In what ways is SoloTrek different from the device used in the James Bond film?
6. What advantages does SoloTrek have over motorbikes and scooters?
7. How expensive will it be to buy a SoloTrek?
8. Can you buy a SoloTrek now?

4 Look at the text again, who or what do the words in bold refer to?
1. we asked one of **its** inventors to tell us about it. (line 7)
2. It's funny you should mention **that**, because … (line 23)
3. a similar device strapped to **his** back. (line 25)
4. **it** was so incredibly noisy … (line 27)
5. but **it's** only really suitable for short distances. (line 34)

5 Explain the meaning of the phrases from the text.
1. a dream come true (line 1)
2. It's funny you should mention that … (line 23)
3. it's the victim of its own success (line 32)
4. keeps you fit (line 34)

DISCUSSION

6 Discuss the questions.
1. What are the advantages and disadvantages of the SoloTrek?
2. If you could afford it, would you buy a SoloTrek? Why / Why not?
3. Can you think of any other inventions that would be useful in the future?

58   Unit 7

A dream come true

It's a dream come true. It's an invention as important as the car. It's a one-person flying machine that can take off vertically, get you to your destination above the traffic jams and then land vertically, almost anywhere. It's light, it's compact, and it only takes a few hours to learn how to fly it. It's the SoloTrek XFV. It's being developed in California, and we asked one of its inventors to tell us about it.

How fast and how far can it fly? About 130 kph, and it'll be able to fly at that speed for 1½ hours.

And how high? Most flights will probably be at a height of about 30 metres, in other words just above the tops of trees, but high enough to give you a great view of the traffic jams below. If you wanted, though, you could climb to 100 metres.

What would happen if the engine suddenly stopped? No problem, unless you were really unlucky! If something was wrong with its engine, you'd get lots of warning and you'd land safely. But if you made a mistake, you could use SoloTrek's built-in parachute.

Is SoloTrek really a new invention? It's funny you should mention that, because in one of the James Bond films, Bond flew with a similar device strapped to his back. So it's not exactly new, but that 'aircraft' could only fly for a maximum of 30 seconds, and it was so incredibly noisy that they had to take the noise out of the film!

What makes SoloTrek better than other kinds of transport? Well, a lot of people think the car is the most convenient way of travelling. But nowadays it's the victim of its own success. There are so many cars that we spend most of the time stuck in traffic jams. The bike doesn't cause any pollution and keeps you fit, but it's only really suitable for short distances. Motorbikes and scooters are practical for some journeys, unless the weather's bad. However, they're also noisy and dangerous. So we think SoloTrek's a great idea.

OK, so how much will a SoloTrek cost? If everything goes according to plan, it'll cost about the same as an expensive sports car.

If I want one, how long will I have to wait? It's certain to be popular, but so far we've only made a prototype. We're doing our best, but you'll just have to be patient …

Unit 7 59

GRAMMAR

FIRST AND SECOND CONDITIONAL

1 Read the sentences and complete the rules. Use *first conditional* or *second conditional*.

First conditional
If you **want** a SoloTrek, it **will cost** about the same as a sports car.

Second conditional
If the engine **stopped**, you **would land** safely.

> We use the _____ to talk about a likely or possible future situation.
> We use the _____ + to talk about an improbable future situation.

NOTE!
Look at the word order in these examples. The sentences have the same meaning.

If something was wrong, you'd get lots of warning.
You'd get lots of warning if something was wrong.

2 Match the two parts of the sentences.
1 If I have enough money
2 I'd buy a sports car
3 If I was a multi-millionaire
4 I'll continue to go by bus
5 If the bus comes soon
6 I'd be surprised

a if I had a lot of money.
b if it's cheaper than going by car.
c I won't be late.
d I'll buy a scooter next year.
e if it came on time.
f I'd buy a private jet.

UNLESS

3 Read the sentence and choose the correct meaning.
SoloTrek is a dream come true **unless** you have a lot of luggage.

> *Unless* means the same as:
> A *also* or *as well as*.
> B *but*.
> C *except if …* or *if … not*.

4 Rewrite these sentences using *unless*.
If it doesn't rain I'll travel by bike.
I'll travel by bike unless it rains.
1 If I don't become rich, I won't buy a SoloTrek.
2 If you don't lend me some money, I won't finish my research.
3 If my invention doesn't work, nobody will buy it.
4 If you don't concentrate, you won't understand.
5 I won't explain how it works if you don't listen.
6 She's always on time if she doesn't get stuck in traffic jams.

5 Complete the text. Use the first or second conditional.

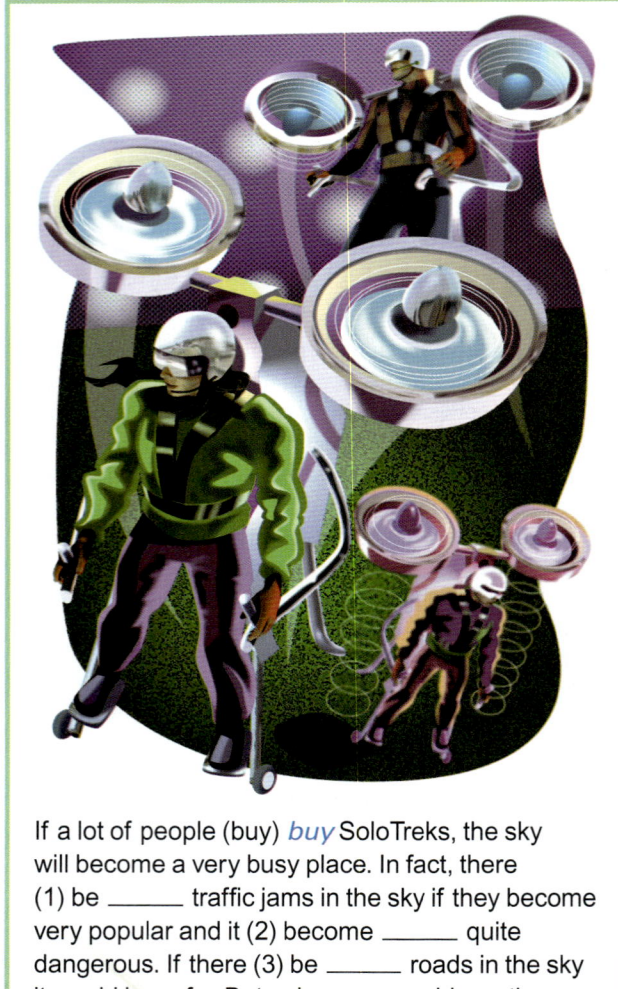

If a lot of people (buy) *buy* SoloTreks, the sky will become a very busy place. In fact, there (1) be _____ traffic jams in the sky if they become very popular and it (2) become _____ quite dangerous. If there (3) be _____ roads in the sky it would be safer. But unless you could see the road, how (4) know _____ you _____ you were on it? And where (5) put _____ they _____ traffic lights? But it (6) solve _____ the traffic problems of big cities if everybody had a SoloTrek. People (7) fly _____ to work so there wouldn't be so many cars on the roads. But unless they invent a SoloTrek with four seats they (8) not be _____ much use for people with families.

6 Complete the sentences about you.
1 If I had enough money I …
2 If I was an inventor …
3 If public transport was free …
4 If the world's oil reserves run out …
5 If we discover an alternative source of energy …

7 Compare your ideas with a partner.

Grammar reference page 107

VOCABULARY

MAKE AND DO

1 Read the sentences and then complete the table. Use the words in the box.

A I **made** a **decision**.
B We're **doing** our **best**.

> a decision   your best   an excuse   damage
> harm   an effort   an impression   a suggestion
> work   a difference   a change   a favour   a copy
> research

MAKE	DO
a decision	_____
_____	_____
_____	_____
_____	_____
_____	_____
_____	_____

NOTE!
It's a good idea to learn words that go together. This makes them easier to remember.
make a decision; do your best

2 Complete the sentences. Use the correct form of *make* or *do*.

1 You're not _____ enough work. Stop _____ excuses and _____ an effort instead.
2 Can I _____ a suggestion? Why don't you invent something useful, something that will really _____ a difference to people's lives and not _____ any damage to the environment?
3 He took his new invention to the manufacturers and he _____ a good impression. He's now waiting for them to _____ a decision.
4 Just _____ your best. Unless your experiment goes badly wrong, it won't _____ any harm.

3 Do you have different words for *make* and *do* in your language?

IDIOMS

4 Match sentences (1–6) with the definitions (a–f).

1 Many inventors **go to great lengths** to sell their inventions. They often travel all over the world to show them to different companies.
2 The engineers experienced great problems developing the SoloTrek, but they **took** everything **in their stride** and searched for solutions.
3 We **take** a lot of inventions **for granted**. We can't even imagine life without them.
4 The police investigation **brought** some very suspicious practices **to light**.
5 He's **made up his mind**. He wants to be an inventor.
6 'I can't decide for you. It's **up to you**.'

a your decision or responsibility
b face difficult situations or problems calmly
c not to appreciate something properly
d come to a decision
e make a big effort to do something
f reveal some unknown information or news

5 Complete the sentences about you.
1 I sometimes go to great lengths to …
2 I take _____ in my stride.
3 I don't take _____ for granted.
4 _____ is up to me.
5 I find it hard to make my mind up when …
6 I recently read in the papers that _____ had been brought to light.

6 Compare your ideas with a partner.

Unit 7   61

READING

1 Read the text. For questions 1–4, choose the correct answer A, B or C.

1. If William C Lowe and his team hadn't invented the PC,
   A the Internet would have become very popular.
   B mass-market computers wouldn't have been available.
   C millions of people would have bought their own computers.

2. If businesses hadn't bought computers for their offices,
   A the industry would have been the fourth largest in the world.
   B our ways of working and communicating would be very different.
   C new technology would have developed very quickly.

3. If text messaging hadn't been invented,
   A teenagers wouldn't have discovered a new way of communicating.
   B parents and teachers wouldn't have understood it.
   C predictive text would have become popular.

4. If predictive text hadn't arrived in 1999,
   A young people wouldn't have used text messaging.
   B adults would have learnt it.
   C text messaging wouldn't have developed so fast.

2 Match the words with the definitions.

1. decade (line 11)
2. transformed (line 11)
3. predicted (line 13)
4. spread (line 17)
5. instant (line 28)
6. device (line 38)
7. adapted (line 42)

a changed completely
b changed so it could be used more easily
c reached more and more people
d immediate; very fast
e a piece of equipment made for a specific purpose
f said they thought something will happen
g ten years

3 Explain the meaning of the phrases.

1. came to life (line 6)
2. one-to-one communication (line 28)
3. came on the market (line 38)
4. as their own (line 42)

Inventions that changed the world

At 10 a.m. on 12th August 1981, a small group of American inventors calling themselves the Dirty Dozen and led by William C. Lowe met in Florida. Lowe flicked
5 a switch and they all cheered as a small screen came to life. The first cheap, easy to use, mass-market computer had been born.

IBM called its new invention the PC, short for personal computer. It had only 15 kilobytes of
10 memory and it cost a huge $1,565. But within two decades it has transformed the way we work, talk, write, relax and, above all, communicate. IBM predicted that it would sell 241,683 PCs. They were hopelessly and
15 completely wrong. In the next 15 years they sold over 500 million. No other invention or technology has spread so fast. Today almost every office in the world and millions of homes have their own PC. As a result the computer
20 industry has become the fourth biggest industry in the world after energy, cars and crime. If that first PC hadn't worked, the world would have developed very differently.

How often do you send or get text messages? If you're a typical teenager, the answer's probably 'several times a day'.
25 According to Alex (17) from London, 'I don't know what I'd do without text messaging. It's instant and convenient one-to-one communication. It costs
30 me next to nothing compared to the cost of talking on a mobile.' The fact is, teenagers wouldn't have developed a whole new trendy way of
35 communicating, if text messaging hadn't been invented. It all started on September 10th 1996 when the world's first two-way text messaging device came on the market. But it wouldn't have become so popular if predictive text,
40 which guesses what you're going to write, hadn't arrived in 1999. Since then teenagers have used and adapted the text message as their own. Some adults find it difficult to understand messages like CU 2nite (See you
45 tonight) and RU free 2moro B4 8? (Are you free tomorrow before eight?) and that's part of its attraction for young people.

So, the next time you use a PC or send a text message, remember William C Lowe and the
50 Dirty Dozen and the inventors of the first SMS (Short Message Service). You might not have thought about it before, but these inventions have changed the world.

GRAMMAR

THIRD CONDITIONAL

1 Read the sentences and complete the rule. Use *past perfect* and *have*.

If that first PC **hadn't worked**, the world **would have developed** very differently.

> We form the third conditional with *If* + _____ + *would(n't)* + _____ + past participle.

2 Choose the correct alternative.
1 We use the third conditional to talk about something in
   A the future.
   B the present.
   C the past.
2 We use the third conditional to talk about
   A something that really happened in the past.
   B imaginary or hypothetical situations in the past.

3 Complete the sentences. Use the third conditional.

1 Nobody (design) _____ computer games if Lowe and the Dirty Dozen (not build) _____ the first personal computer.
2 If PlayStation 2 (not be) _____ so popular, there (not be) _____ a world shortage of microchips in 2000.
3 If only children (play) _____ on Play Stations, Sony (not sell) _____ so many.
4 If adults (not start) _____ buying computer games they (remain) _____ childrens' toys.
5 A lot of people (become) _____ bored with computer games if the computer graphics (not be) _____ so good.

4 Read the text and complete the sentences below.

The inventor George Eastman

George Eastman was born in New York in 1854. His parents weren't rich so he left school when he was only 14. He was always interested in photography and a few years later he invented his first camera. He was a brilliant inventor and next he invented the first roll of film. A few years later he made the first Kodak camera and this revolutionized the popularity of photography. The Kodak camera was very cheap and practical, which meant that millions of people bought cameras for the first time. Eastman was a good businessman and he made a fortune from his inventions. In fact he made so much money he gave away over $100 million.

If Eastman's parents had been rich he (not leave) … .

If Eastman's parents had been rich he wouldn't have left school when he was only 14.

1 If Eastman hadn't been interested in photography, (not invent) …
2 He wouldn't have invented the roll film if (not be) …
3 If Eastman hadn't invented the Kodak camera, photography (become) …
4 Millions of people wouldn't have bought a camera for the first time if (not be) …
5 If Eastman hadn't been a good businessman, (make) …
6 He wouldn't have given away $100 million if (make) …

5 Answer the questions.
1 What language would you have learnt if you hadn't studied English?
2 If you'd had the choice, would you have gone to a different school?
3 What would have happened if you'd been late for school today?
4 If you'd been born ten years earlier, how would your life have been different?

Grammar reference page 107

Unit 7   63

VOCABULARY

SYNONYMS

1 Complete the lists with adjectives with similar meanings.

> convenient revolutionary popular trendy
> practical adaptable essential original
> flexible smart innovative adjustable

WAYS OF DESCRIBING INVENTIONS	
Useful	Fashionable
convenient	_____
_____	_____
_____	_____
Imaginative	Versatile
_____	_____
_____	_____
_____	_____

2 Choose the correct alternative.
1 It's not very *smart / convenient*. It's too heavy to carry around and it's awkward to use.
2 It's really *flexible / innovative*. Nobody's ever thought of anything like it before.
3 You don't really need one. You only bought it because it's *revolutionary / trendy* at the moment.
4 They've become *imaginative / essential*. Everybody thinks they've just got to have one.
5 Anybody can use them. It doesn't matter how tall you are because they're *original / adjustable*.
6 I don't care that young people think it's *fashionable / adaptable*. I just want to be sure that it's *practical / popular* and it works.

3 Discuss the questions.
1 What's the most popular model of mobile phone in your class?
2 What's the most original piece of music that you've heard recently?
3 Do you think that owning a car is essential these days, or is there a convenient alternative?
4 Have you ever bought anything that was trendy at the time, but which isn't trendy any more? What was it?
5 What controls can you adjust on TVs and radios?

LISTENING

4 Listen to the descriptions of various inventions. Which inventions are being described? Choose from the inventions in the pictures. 🎧

5 Listen again, and answer the questions.

Invention 1: Where are you usually sitting when you use this invention?
Invention 2: This invention is more practical and convenient than something. What?
Invention 3: When do you not wear this invention?
Invention 4: What do you need if you haven't got this invention with you?
Invention 5: What can you watch if you have this invention?

SPEAKING

6 Guess what it is.
a Work in groups. Each member of the group chooses an important invention of the last 100 years.
b Take it in turns to describe your invention. Say why you think it's important, what it looks like, and how and when it's used.
c Other members of the group ask questions and guess what the invention is.

Have you got one?
Are they very expensive?
Are they very trendy at the moment?

64 Unit 7

WRITING

PLANNING

1 Read the magazine article. What is the invention?

Innovations

Brushing your teeth – boring but necessary? Inventor Carl Appleby got so fed up with it that he decided to do something about it one morning. We asked Carl to tell us more about his revolutionary new invention.

What was your idea exactly? I've invented a transparent protective paint for your teeth. It's very practical because it means that you won't need toothbrushes, toothpaste or even a dentist ever again.

It sounds really innovative. Yes, it's exciting, isn't it? And I think it'll become very popular.

How far have you got? Well, if it all goes according to plan, I'm hoping it'll be on sale next year. I'm going to advertise it in magazines like yours.

How much will it cost? It'll be more expensive than toothpaste, but much cheaper than going to the dentist!

So that's something that everyone can look forward to buying and using before too long.

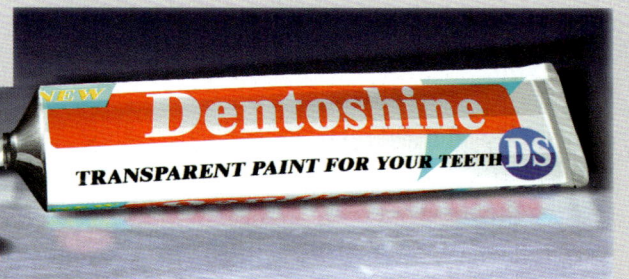

2 What adjectives do the inventor and the journalist use to describe the invention?

3 You are going to write a 120–150 word magazine article about a new invention. Think of an invention which you think would be very useful, or use one of the inventions from this unit.

4 Plan your article. Write a short introduction and an imaginary interview with the inventor to find out:
- What is it?
- Why is it such a good idea?
- What advantages does it have over earlier inventions?
- How does it work?
- How much will it cost?
- When will it be ready?
- How does the inventor plan to sell it?

5 Write your article using the plan to help you. Include the information from your interview, and some of the adjectives from the Vocabulary section on page 64.

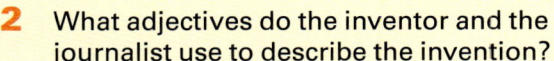

Introduction
What is the problem?

Interview questions and answers
Use your notes from Exercise 4.

Conclusion
Why is it a good invention?

8 First impressions

INTRODUCTION

1 Look at the pictures and answer the questions. How would you describe the people, their hair and their clothes? Use the words in the box to help you.

| leather | pierced | plastic | denim | checked |
| dreadlocks | spiky | dyed | greasy | shaved |

He's a young man with shaved hair and a moustache. He's wearing a colourful waistcoat and checked trousers. He doesn't look very friendly.

2 Imagine you are on a crowded bus. The only seats left are next to these people. Who would you sit next to? Why?

I'd sit next to the man with the leather jacket. He looks like he's keen on motorbikes, and I like motorbikes, too.

READING

3 You are going to read a text about skateboarding. Before you read, list the things you already know about the topic.

Skateboarding:
- *Skateboarding is becoming more popular.*
- *Some skaters wear helmets.*

4 Read the text. Which things on your list are mentioned?

5 Read the text again and answer the questions.
1 How do we know that skateboarding is popular?
2 What is the name of the London skateboarding championship?
3 At the championship, who are the main competitors?
4 Why do people like skateboarding clothes?
5 Where did people skate before there were skate parks?
6 What were skateboards originally used for?
7 Why do dedicated skaters often get injured?
8 Why does skateboarding appeal to young people?

6 Find words in the text with similar meanings to:

Paragraph A
1 show a television programme
2 most recent
3 to find out about something

Paragraph B
4 talk in a friendly way
5 for everybody

Paragraph C
6 a dangerous activity that someone does to entertain people

7 Explain the meaning of the phrases.
1 take it in turns (line 18)
2 a way of getting around (line 34)
3 it doesn't seem to matter (line 50)

DISCUSSION

8 Discuss the questions.
1 Do people skateboard in your town?
2 Have you ever tried skateboarding?
3 Do you think skateboarding is fun?
4 What do you and your friends think about skateboarding fashion?

66 Unit 8

STREET LIFE

A Image isn't just about what you wear, it's also about what you do in your free time and who your friends are. Perhaps that's why skateboarding is so popular. Nowadays there are skate parks in most cities, sports channels which broadcast skateboarding competitions, and websites that sell the latest equipment. It's even starting to affect the clothes that people wear. So what's the big attraction? Journalist Zoe Wells went to London's skateboarding championships to check it out.

B At the G-Shock Skate Jam, where skateboarders compete every year, groups of trendy teenagers stand around in the sunshine. Most of the boys take it in turns to skate and compete with one another while the girls chat and watch them. Almost everyone is wearing big baggy trousers, cut-off T-shirts and chunky trainers. 'Anyone can skateboard,' explains a girl whose brother is competing. 'And anyone can wear the clothes – they look cool on girls as well as boys.' The clothes then, like the sport, are universal. Perhaps that's why so many people are keen on it.

C Skateboards were originally invented in the 1970s. Wherever there was a pavement, you could skate, and the teenagers who bought those first skateboards used them as a means of transport. Today, however, they're much more than a way of getting around – they're a way of life. 'Skateboarding has a radical image,' explains Max, who is a professional skateboarder. 'It's all about freedom, having confidence in yourself and pushing things to the limit.' And skate jams often push things to the limit. The action is fast-paced and the stunts are often dangerous. Dedicated skaters often hurt their arms and legs while they're doing them.

D However, you don't have to go fast or do high jumps to enjoy skateboarding. 'You need to be experienced and confident to compete in skate jams,' says Max, 'but you don't have to be a professional to skate.' At the skate park and on the city streets there are beginners and pros, girls as well as boys. It doesn't seem to matter who you are or how good you are. As long as you have a board and the right attitude, you belong.

Unit 8 67

GRAMMAR

DEFINING RELATIVE CLAUSES

1 Read the sentences and complete the rules. Use *which*, *that*, *where*, *who* and *whose*.

a There are sports channels **which** broadcast skateboarding competitions.
b Skateboarding is starting to affect the clothes **that** people wear.
c That's the place **where** teenagers skateboard.
d There are lots of people **who** can't skate well.
e There's the girl **whose** brother is competing.

> Defining relative clauses give information and help us to identify someone or something.
> We use:
> 1 _____ or _____ for people.
> 2 _____ or _____ for things.
> 3 _____ for places.
> 4 _____ for possession.

2 Rewrite the sentences. Use *that*, *who*, *which*, *whose* and *where*.

Matt has got a new skateboard. It's very fast.
Matt has got a new skateboard *which is very fast*.

1 At the skate jam there were girls. They were competing.
   At the skate jam there were girls …
2 That's the skate park. I used to practise there.
   That's the skate park …
3 I talked to a boy. His brother is an athlete.
   I talked to a boy …
4 Professionals use special skateboards. They cost over £100.
   Professionals use special skateboards …
5 I bought a skateboard. I had seen it in a shop.
   I bought a skateboard …
6 That's my friend Martine. She works for a sports channel.
   That's my friend Martine …
7 Justin bought a computer game. He plays it most evenings.
   Justin bought a computer game …

3 Complete the text. Use *that*, *who*, *which*, *whose* or *where*.

Modern crazes: the micro scooter

It's the latest thing to appear on the streets – a small scooter *which* is made of aluminium and is light and easy to carry. It's called the micro scooter and it was invented by a man (1) _____ friends used to laugh when he rode it!

Today there are lots of city people (2) _____ use micro scooters. It's a form of transport (3) _____ is quick and easy to use. In Japan, the place (4) _____ most people use their scooters is in underground subway stations. In some European cities, there are special Micro stops (5) _____ scooters are rented by the hour. But it's not just for city commuters. There are also sports versions (6) _____ are popular with teenagers too!

4 Write beginnings for the sentences.

The clothes which I bought for the party shrank when I washed them!

1 _____ I used to watch on TV has finished.
2 _____ skateboard I borrowed is in my class.
3 _____ we used to go after school has become a clothes shop.
4 _____ played football with my brother now plays for A.C. Milan.
5 _____ normally leaves at 5 p.m. will leave at 5.15 today.

Grammar reference page 108

68 Unit 8

VOCABULARY

DESCRIBING APPEARANCE

1 Match the descriptions to the people.
1. Liam is **short**, **tanned** and **good-looking**. He's fairly **stocky** and he's got **long, straight** hair.
2. Jordan is **tall** with **short dark** hair. He's **slim** and **athletic**, and he looks very **trendy**. ___
3. Sean is **medium-height** and **well-built**. He's got **freckles**, and is quite **pale**. He's also got **ginger, wavy** hair. ___

2 Complete the lists. Use the words from Exercise 1.

> Height: *short*
> Build: *stocky*
> Hair: *long*
> Complexion: *tanned*
> General appearance: *trendy*

3 Add these words to the lists. Use a dictionary to help you.

> plain sporty bald plaits pony-tail
> overweight skinny spiky curly spotty
> wrinkled untidy

4 Complete the description. Use adjectives from Exercises 2 and 3.

My best friend Clare is a professional skateboarder. I've known her for three years and we first met at a skate park in London. The first thing you notice about Clare is her hair. It's (1 hair) _____ and a bit (2 hair) _____ and very pink. Then you notice her fantastic eyes!

Clare's quite tall and fairly (3 build) _____ . She looks great in most things because she's extremely (4 general appearance) _____ .

She's also quite (5 complexion) _____ , so she wears a lot of make-up, but she doesn't really need to.

5 Write a short description of someone you know well. It could be a friend, someone famous or a member of your family.
- Use adjectives to make your description interesting.
- Use adverbs such as *a bit*, *quite*, and *fairly* to make your description accurate.

Unit 8

READING

1 Read the text and match the topics (1–4) with the paragraphs (A–D).
1 The origins of the Doc Marten boot.
2 The continued success of Doc Martens.
3 How the Doc Marten image developed.
4 Doc Martens have been worn in many different ways.

2 Find evidence in the text to support the sentences.

Some people paint their Doc Martens.
People have painted flowers on them … and dyed them red, white and blue.

1 People can wear Doc Martens with different types of clothes.
2 Doc Martens have surprising origins.
3 Klaus invented the Doc Marten boot to help him walk.
4 Doc Martens were originally popular with workers.
5 Punk rockers changed the image of Doc Martens.
6 Many different kinds of people have worn Doc Martens.

3 Find words or phrases in the text which match the definitions.

Paragraph A
1 made something a different colour
Paragraph B
2 moving from one place to another
3 something that hurts you
Paragraph C
4 not doing what society wants you to do
5 stronger, harder

4 Discuss the questions.
1 Doc Martens have been worn by everyone, including teenagers and adults. How are today's teenage and adult fashions similar?
2 How are they different?

The Doc Marten Story

A They're shoes that are worn by everyone – from supermodels to the Dalai Lama. Pop stars *Aqua* have a pair, and so do film stars like Johnny Depp. People have painted flowers on them, worn them with jeans and designer dresses, and dyed them red, white and
5 blue. There's even a pop song about them. What are they? They're Doc Marten boots.

B Doc Martens are as much a part of British culture as drinking tea, but strangely enough they were invented by a German! It all started in the 1940s when Dr Klaus Maertens, who was on holiday
10 in the Alps, had a skiing accident. Klaus, whose foot was badly broken, had problems getting around. Walking was so painful that he made a special pair of shoes from old car tyres. These shoes, which were ugly but comfortable, became the original Dr Maertens' boots. Two years later he started selling the new boots. But it
15 wasn't until 1959 that a British shoemaker bought them. He changed the name to Doc Martens – the name on a million feet!

C In the early days, when Doc Martens first started, postmen, factory workers and policemen bought them. But in the 1970s and 80s the boots' image changed. Groups such as punk rockers, whose image
20 was wild and rebellious, began to wear them. Hard-wearing Docs became a symbol of alienation, and boots with a lot of holes became very trendy – the bigger your boots, the tougher you were. In fact the biggest boots ever made were worn by the popstar Elton John. They were specially designed for a film called *Tommy* and they were
25 an amazing 1m 30cm high!

D Today Doc Martens are universal – from postmen to punk rockers, even politicians wear them! Doc Martens continue to surprise us. Who will be wearing them next?

70 Unit 8

GRAMMAR

NON-DEFINING RELATIVE CLAUSES

1 Read the sentences and answer the questions.
  a Dr Maertens, **who** was on holiday in the Alps, had a skiing accident.
  b These shoes, **which** were ugly but comfortable, became the original Dr Maertens' boots.
  1 Do non-defining relative clauses introduce essential or non-essential information?
  2 Where do we put the commas in non-defining relative clauses?

> **NOTE!**
> We don't use 'that' in non-defining relative clauses.
> *The trainers, ~~that~~ which were fashionable, were too expensive.*

2 Find five examples of non-defining relative clauses with *who*, *when*, *whose* and *where* in the text on page 70.

3 Choose the correct alternative.
  Ella's boots, (which)/ *that* were hand-painted, were very original.
  1 Daniel, *who / whose* sister is a designer, is very trendy.
  2 Holly's T-shirt, *that / which* was orange, looked odd with her jeans.
  3 My father, *who / which* was a postman, used to wear Doc Martens.
  4 The new café, *where / that* I meet my friends, isn't far from here.
  5 Karl, *whose / which* family lives in London, is my penfriend.

4 Complete the second sentence so that it has a similar meaning to the first sentence.
  Paul wears Doc Martens boots. He is a biker.
  Paul, who is a biker, wears Doc Marten's boots.
  1 The tattoo was expensive. It looked quite ugly.
     The tattoo, which …
  2 Karl is my best friend. His brother is an architect.
     Karl, whose …
  3 The Ritz Hotel had a fashion show. The hotel is famous.
     The Ritz Hotel, which …
  4 Ella is very creative. She's studying design.
     Ella, who …
  5 Helen often buys new clothes. She loves shopping.
     Helen, who …
  6 *All Sports* has closed down. I bought my trainers there.
     All Sports, where …

5 Complete the text with the correct clause.
  a whose tattoos have been done by 13 different artists
  b which means 'to mark'
  c which cost an amazing $15,000
  d who travelled all over the world
  e who comes from Canada
  f which were worn by the Egyptians
  g where tattoos had been popular for centuries
  h which were only numbers

Body Art

Tattoos, *which were worn by the Egyptians*, are one of the oldest forms of body decoration. However it wasn't until the 18th century that they arrived in Europe. In 1769 Captain James Cook discovered Polynesia, (1) _____, and brought body art back to England. In fact the word 'tattoo', (2) _____, is a Tahitian word.

In the 18th century, sailors, (3) _____, had tattoos of the places they had visited. Prisoners also had tattoos, although their tattoos, (4) _____, were used to identify them.

Nowadays lots of different people have tattoos, and some people have more than one. Krystyne Kolorful, (5) _____, has covered all her body with tattoos. Her expensive body art, (6) _____, took 10 years to complete. Not surprisingly, Krystyne, (7) _____, loves looking different. 'Tattoos are an amazing way to express yourself,' she says.

6 Complete these sentences in your own words.
  1 My favourite CD, which …
  2 My old school, where …
  3 The last book I read, which …
  4 My English teacher, who …
  5 My best friend, who …
  6 Our local café, where …

Grammar reference page 108

Unit 8   71

VOCABULARY

PHRASAL VERBS: TAKE

1 Read the text and match the phrasal verbs with the descriptions.

When Laura met Karl she immediately (1) **took to him**. He (2) **took after** his older brother and was tall and good-looking. All the girls liked him. Then one day Karl offered to (3) **take her out** to the cinema. It was a dream come true, but what could she wear? At first she bought a skirt, but it was too long. She couldn't (4) **take it up**, so she (5) **took it back** to the shop. Then she bought some jeans and a trendy skateboarding T-shirt. They looked great!

The big day arrived and Karl came in and (6) **took off** his jacket. Unfortunately he was wearing exactly the same T-shirt. How embarrassing!

a   remove clothing
b   behave or look like someone
c   return something
d   like someone you meet for the first time
e   shorten something
f   go somewhere with someone

2 Complete the sentences with the correct form of the phrasal verbs from Exercise 1.

1   Tanya _____ her mother. She has the same blonde hair and blue eyes.
2   'It's too hot in here!'
    'Why don't you _____ your coat?'
3   'These rollerblades are too small. I'll have to _____ them _____.'
4   Dave wanted to _____ Jenna _____ to a disco, but he was too shy to ask.
5   Rachel _____ Tina as soon as she met her. She was really friendly.
6   Susie had to _____ her trousers. They were far too long.

LISTENING

3 Listen to the first part of the conversation about image. What are Jody and Richard doing?

4 Listen to the second part of the conversation. What are Richard's answers to the questions?

1   How often do you go clothes shopping? _____
2   Do you often take things back to the shop? _____
3   How much time do you spend getting ready to go out? _____
4   Which would you prefer to read – a sports magazine or a fashion magazine? _____
5   How often do you get your hair cut? _____
6   Which do you prefer – comfortable clothes or fashionable clothes? _____

PRONUNCIATION

5 Listen to how the word is pronounced. Which letters are not pronounced?
comfortable

6 Listen and repeat. Mark the letters which are not pronounced.
1   fashionable
2   dictionary
3   different
4   restaurant
5   interesting
6   definitely
7   favourite

SPEAKING

7 How image-conscious are you? Ask your partner the questions from Listening Exercise 4. Use the phrases to help you.

Useful phrases
That's easy!
I'd definitely say …
I suppose …
I'm not sure, but …
I used to … but now
… about once / twice / three times a month

Unit 8

WRITING

FORMAL LETTERS

1 Listen to the conversation. Where does it take place? What is the problem?

2 Read the letter of complaint. Who is the letter written to? What does the writer want?

> 34 Canterbury Road
> Bristol
> BS5 4NP
> 17 October 2003
>
> Dear Sir / Madam
>
> A I am writing to complain about a pair of trousers which I recently bought from Star Shops. I was very pleased with the trousers until I tried to wash them. Unfortunately the dye ran and (1) *now I really can't go out in them / as a result I can no longer wear them.*
>
> B When I (2) *returned the trousers / took the stuff back to the shop,* the shop assistant was (3) *really horrible / extremely unhelpful.* At first she suggested that I hadn't read the washing instructions. Then she called the manager. The manager said that there had been no other complaints and (4) *refused to give me a refund. / wouldn't give me my money back!*
>
> C I am very disappointed in Star Shops as I am a good customer. (5) *It'd be really good / I would therefore appreciate it* if you could either replace the trousers or send me a full refund. Please find enclosed a copy of my receipt.
>
> (6) *I look forward to hearing from you. / Write soon!*
>
> Yours faithfully
>
> *Michelle Tims*

3 Read the letter again. Match the paragraph topics (1–3) with the paragraphs (A–C).
1 what the writer wants now
2 the reason for writing
3 how the shop responded

4 Look at the letter again. Find 1–6 in the text. Choose the alternative that is more formal.

> **NOTE!**
>
> **Letter writing**
> Before you start writing, think about:
> • who you are writing to. Do you know the person? Should your letter be formal or informal?
> • why you are writing. What do you want them to do?
> • the layout of your letter. Make sure you put the date and address in the correct place.

5 Read the advertisement and the comments. Write a letter of complaint (120–150 words). Use the paragraph plan to help you.

Multimix MP3 player

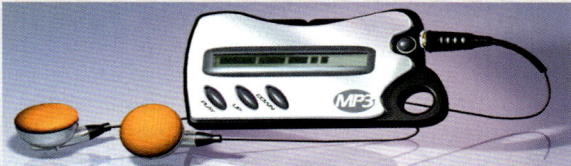

- stores up to 5 hours of music *I only got 2 hours*
- top quality sound
- automatic playback
- free DJ software *doesn't work!*

To order write to:
Multimix players Ltd., 6 North Road, London NW6
or contact customer services on: *very unhelpful!*
0156 4563 768

Paragraph 1: Say why you are writing.
When did you buy the MP3 player? What was the problem?

Paragraph 2: Explain how the problem was dealt with.
Did you phone customer services? What did they say?

Paragraph 3: Say what you want.
Do you want a replacement or a refund?

Unit 8

Units 7–8: revision

GRAMMAR

CONDITIONAL SENTENCES

1 Match the two parts of the sentences.

1 If it's fine tomorrow
2 If I had enough money
3 I'll ask Dan to come with us
4 If you work hard
5 I'd come with you
6 I wouldn't go

a you'll pass the exam.
b we'll go to the beach.
c if I didn't have so much homework.
d if I didn't have to.
e I'd buy a new leather jacket.
f if you want.

2 Read the text and then complete the sentences.

> The Japanese Sony company decided to give their first games console an English name – PlayStation – because they wanted to sell a lot of them in the USA. They gave hundreds of PlayStations to DJs and sports stars, and in this way they got a lot of free publicity. It was a huge success because adults as well children enjoyed playing with them.
>
> When PlayStation 2 arrived in 2000, over a million were sold in the first three days, and there was an instant worldwide shortage of microchips. Sony have deliberately kept the price of PlayStation 2 at $199.99 in the USA, and this has helped them to sell over 100 million PlayStations. More than one in three American households has a PlayStation, and as a result the word has become part of the English language.

Sony (not sell) *wouldn't have sold* so many PlayStations in the USA if *they hadn't decided to give it an English name*.
1 They (not get) _____ a lot of free publicity if …
2 It (not be) _____ a huge success if adults …
3 If Sony (not sell) _____ over 1 million PlayStation 2's in three days there …
4 If Sony (not keep) _____ the price of PlayStations below $200 …
5 If one in three American households (not buy) _____ a PlayStation …

3 Complete the sentences. Use first, second or third conditionals.

1 I'll phone you on my mobile if …
2 If you send me a text message …
3 I won't contact you unless …

4 If I had my own computer …
5 I'd have it in my bedroom unless …
6 I'd surf the net if …

7 I'd have bought a PlayStation if …
8 If my brother had let me use his …
9 I wouldn't have wanted one unless …

RELATIVE CLAUSES

4 Rewrite the sentences. Use *that, who, which, whose* and *where*.

That's the pop star. She plays rock music. (who)
That's the pop star who plays rock music.

1 That's the inventor. He invented microscooters. (who)
2 This is the factory. They make personal computers here. (where)
3 That's the red jacket. The TV presenter wore it. (which)
4 That's the boy. His sister designs clothes. (whose)
5 The café is near the shop. I bought a DVD player from the shop. (where)
6 That's the designer. She makes very stylish aluminium chairs. (who)

5 Rewrite the sentences. Add a non-defining relative clause with the word in brackets.

My sister spends all her money on clothes. (who)
My sister, *who is two years older than me*, spends all her money on clothes.
1 Some of her clothes are quite expensive. (which)
2 Her best friend is also crazy about clothes. (whose)
3 On Saturdays they always go shopping together. (when)
4 The Internet café is in the centre of town. (where)
5 My brother isn't interested in clothes. (who)

VOCABULARY

MAKE AND DO

1 Rewrite the words in bold with a phrase using *make* or *do* + a noun. Use the nouns in the box.

> decision effort difference excuse damage suggestion an impression

You must **decide**. Which jeans are you going to buy?
You must make a decision. Which jeans are you going to buy?

1 I'd like to **give you advice about what to do**. Why don't you change your hairstyle?
2 Lisa doesn't care what she looks like. She should **try hard** to look smarter.
3 Don't **try to explain your bad behaviour**. It was wrong.
4 It **changes things** if you wear make-up.
5 As soon as Sophie walks into the room she **has an effect on other people**.
6 He forgot to put oil in the car but it didn't **cause anything to be broken or harmed**.

IDIOMS

2 Match the two parts of the sentences.

1 She goes to great lengths to look nice
2 He took his disappointment in his stride
3 She took it for granted
4 We brought to light
5 He hasn't made up his mind

a and started again.
b some faults in the design.
c because he hasn't had enough time to decide
d and takes a lot of trouble over her clothes
e that her business would succeed eventually.

SYNONYMS

3 Complete the sentences. Use the words in the box.

> trendy adjustable adaptable essential revolutionary

1 The Multicom phone is very _____. You can use it in lots of different ways.
2 The Cyclotron exercise bike is not as _____ as its inventor claims. Other people have already come up with similar designs.
3 The Multistar DVD player is very _____ at the moment. A lot of pop stars have got one.
4 Everybody should have safety belts in their car. They're _____ nowadays, even in the back seat.
5 It doesn't matter how tall or short you are. The Personal Desktop is fully _____.

4 Complete the notes using the words in the box.

> slim tanned stocky spotty ginger pony-tail
> frizzy pale brown freckles

Beth
Build: _____
Face and complexion:
_____ _____
Hair: _____ _____

Gemma
Build: _____
Face and complexion:
_____ _____
Hair: _____ _____

5 Complete the text. Use the words from Exercise 4.

> These are my two friends, Beth and Gemma. Beth always looks (1) _____ compared to Gemma who has a (2) _____ complexion. Beth has got (3) _____ on her face but she doesn't like them. Gemma's face is a bit (4) _____, but she's not interested in how she looks. Beth is quite (4) _____ – she only weighs 55 kilos. Gemma, on the other hand, is quite (5) _____ – she must weigh over 70 kilos. Beth's hair is (6) _____ and she usually wears it in a (7) _____, whereas Gemma's got (8) _____, (9) _____ hair.

PHRASAL VERBS: *TAKE*

6 Complete the sentences to show that you understand the meaning of the phrasal verbs.

Max **took off** his coat because *it was so hot.*

1 Joe **took off** his shoes because …
2 Hannah didn't **take to** Tim when she first met him because…
3 Pete only **took** Jenny **out** once because …
4 It's easy to see that Jessica **takes after** her mother because …
5 I'm going to **take** this **back** to the shop where I bought it because …
6 I'm going to **take up** this skirt because …

> Now look at the song on page 97.

Revision 7–8

9 Travellers' tales

Introduction

1 Discuss the questions.

1 What are the forms of transport in the pictures? Name five other forms of transport.
2 Which form of transport do you use most often?
3 Which have you never used?
4 Which is the most and which is the least dangerous?
5 Which is the most enjoyable? Why?

Reading

2 Look at the text. Where do you think it comes from?

a a newspaper
b a letter
c a diary

3 Read the text and match the pictures with the days. There are two pictures for one of the days.

Day	Picture(s)
Monday	
Tuesday	
Wednesday	

4 Read the text again and answer the questions.

1 Why did they have to get to Perth?
2 Why was the journey so uncomfortable?
3 What danger did they face?
4 Where was the garage?
5 Why did they only drive for 20 minutes at a time?
6 What was their average speed for the journey?

5 Find the words in the text. For questions 1–5, choose the correct definition.

1 calculated (line 4)
   A worked out
   B guessed
   C saw
2 suburbs (line 7)
   A parks and gardens in a town
   B roads and streets in a town
   C areas outside the centre of a town
3 gateway (line 15)
   A road
   B exit
   C entrance
4 oven (line 20)
   A kitchen
   B bathroom
   C cooker
5 emerged (line 23)
   A spoke
   B stood up
   C came out

6 Explain the meaning of the phrases.

1 went on and on (line 7)
2 We didn't have any choice (line 32)
3 we took it in turns (line 33)

Discussion

7 Discuss the questions.

1 What did you learn about Australia from the text?
2 Do you think they paid a fair price for the petrol? Why / Why not?
3 Would you have taken the kind of risks that they took? Why / Why not?
4 What is the most dangerous journey you've ever made?

The long road west

Monday 2nd February

After three months in Australia we were looking forward to getting back to England. But first we had to get from Sydney to Perth to catch our flight home. I said I wanted to drive across Australia, non-stop. John agreed but then calculated it was 3,800
5 kilometres; the distance from one end of Europe to the other!

Tuesday 3rd February

We set out soon after midnight in a very old Ford, with no air-conditioning. Sydney's suburbs went on and on but then, after we'd crossed the Blue Mountains, the road became flat, straight and very boring.

10 By 7 a.m. it was already getting hot. There were no fences so we had to look out for wild animals crossing the road. Kangaroos can weigh over 100 kilos, and if you hit one at 150 kph both you and the kangaroo will probably be killed! We drove more slowly for a bit.

15 Several hours later we passed a sign which said 'Gateway to Nowhere'. We were entering the Nullarbor Plain. For the next 800 kilometres we saw absolutely nothing; not a tree, not a bush, nothing but desert. It began to get us down. The temperature had now climbed to over 50°C. We opened the windows. It was
20 like opening an oven door. We shut them again. We desperately hoped that we wouldn't break down.

We stopped for more petrol in the middle of the plain. The garage owner emerged from a back room.
'G'day,' I said. 'Can you fill it up?'
25 'Sure,' he replied without a smile. 65 litres disappeared into the tank.
'That'll be 105 dollars,' he said. Now he was smiling.
'You're joking!' I said.
'I'm not,' he said.
30 'How far's the next petrol station?'
'600 kilometres.'
We paid. We didn't have any choice and he knew it.

Wednesday 4th February

We took it in turns to drive, but we were now so tired we could only drive for 20 minutes at a time. We couldn't keep our eyes
35 open for any longer. All we could think about was finishing the journey and sleeping.

In a town called Norseman, we turned right. It was the first time we'd turned the wheel for over 1000 kilometres. Now there were 'only' 800 kilometres to go! We couldn't give up now that
40 we were so 'near'.

Five hours later we saw a big neon sign and some traffic lights. Two hours later we were in the middle of Perth. We'd driven 3,800 kilometres across a whole continent in just under 38 hours.

GRAMMAR

REPORTED SPEECH: STATEMENTS

1 Read the sentences. How do the tenses change?

	Direct speech	Reported speech
a	'I **want** to drive across Australia.'	I said I **wanted** to drive across Australia.
b	'I'm not joking.'	He said he **wasn't** joking.
c	'We **had** a great time.'	He said they **had had** a great time.
d	'We**'ve driven** 3,800 kilometres.'	He said they **had driven** 3,800 kilometres.
e	'It **will cost** over $100.'	He said it **would cost** over $100.

2 Rewrite Sarah's sentences. Use reported speech.

'We've arrived in Turkey.'
She said they had arrived in Turkey.

1 'We flew from London.'
2 'It took four hours.'
3 'We're staying in a cheap hotel.'
4 'It's not far from the beach.'
5 'We eat out every night.'
6 'We've found a fantastic restaurant.'
7 'I don't want to leave.'
8 'We'll stay for another week.'

3 Work in pairs or small groups. Ask and answer the questions.
1 What's the furthest you've ever travelled?
2 Who did you travel with?
3 How did you travel?
4 How long did it take?
5 Was it comfortable?

4 Tell the class what you found out from each other. Use reported speech.

Sam said he had been to New York. He said he went there on holiday with his parents …

TIME EXPRESSIONS IN REPORTED SPEECH

5 Read the sentences and complete the table.
a She said they'd done some sightseeing in Sydney **the week before**.
b He said they'd left Sydney **two days earlier**.
c He said they were going to sleep well **that night**.
d He said their flight home left **the following day**.
e He said they'd arrived home **the day before**.

	Direct speech	Reported speech
1	two days ago	
2	last week	
3	tomorrow	
4	yesterday	
5	tonight	

6 Rewrite the dialogue. Use reported speech.

Tom   We bought this car from you a month ago.
Joe   We went to the coast in it last weekend and it was fine. But it started to go wrong two days ago.
Tom   And yesterday it didn't start.
Joe   It's annoying because we were hoping to use it tonight to go to a party.
Tom   But we can't go, so we want you to repair it.
Mechanic   OK, I'll look at it tomorrow.

Tom said *they had bought that car from him a month earlier.*

Joe said …
Tom added …
Joe explained …
Tom said …
The mechanic said …

Grammar reference page 109

78   Unit 9

Vocabulary

Phrasal verbs: travel

1 Match the phrasal verbs with the definitions.

1	set out	a	to delay
2	look forward to	b	to start a journey
3	break down	c	to enter, go into a vehicle
4	take off	d	to stop working
5	go away	e	to wait with pleasure for something to happen
6	get on	f	to leave home to have a holiday
7	hold up	g	to leave the ground and start flying

2 Complete the text. Use the correct form of the phrasal verbs in Exercise 1.

We hadn't had a holiday for a long time so we decided to (1) _____ for two weeks in July. We were (2) _____ it because it was our first holiday abroad.

We (3) _____ just before 9 o'clock. It wasn't far to the airport but unfortunately we (4) _____ in heavy traffic on the motorway, and then, to make matters far worse, our car (5) _____ . Fortunately there was nothing seriously wrong with the car and we finally arrived at the airport 30 minutes before our flight left. We had to run and we were the last people to (6) _____ the plane. Less than five minutes later it (7) _____ .

Phrasal verbs: get

3 Match the phrasal verbs with the definitions.

1 The water was very warm so I only **got out** of the sea at the end of the day.
2 We had very little money but we **got by** because the food was cheap.
3 We left for France on August 4th and **got back** on August 18th.
4 The weather **got us down** because it rained every day.
5 We **got about** in a car we had hired.
6 We forgot to bring our towels, but we **got away with** it because there were towels in the hotel.
7 I was ill on the first day but I **got over** it and I was fine for the rest of the week.
8 I **got away from** a crowd of tourists by going to the other end of the beach.

a moved from place to place
b managed to live
c made someone depressed
d succeeded in leaving or escaping from somewhere
e left a place
f didn't suffer or be punished for something
g returned
h became better after an unpleasant experience

4 Answer the questions about yourself.
1 When was the last time you got away for a holiday or a break?
2 How do you get about when you're on holiday?
3 What things get you down?
4 When was the last time you got over a bad illness?
5 Do you ever get away with not finishing your homework?

Unit 9   79

READING

1 Read the text. Why do you think it's called *Any excuse*?

Any excuse

A Last week a police patrol car stopped a car on a motorway near Manchester. It was half past two on Saturday afternoon. The car had been driving at over 140 kph, although the motorway was busy and the speed limit is 110 kph.

B Police Constable Burgess said in court that he saw five young men, aged between 18 and 20, in the car. He added that they all seemed extremely impatient to carry on with their journey. He then told the driver to get out of his car, and asked him what his name was. He also asked him if he was in a hurry. 'My name's Lee Bragg,' the driver replied. 'And maybe I was driving a bit too fast, but I can explain why. You see, my car broke down earlier and then I was held up by heavy traffic. I'm in a real hurry now because I'm late for my grandfather's funeral.' PC Burgess then asked the four other young men in the car where they were going. They immediately replied that they were all going to the same funeral. One suggested that they could come to the police station later, if necessary.

C In court PC Burgess said, 'I didn't think they were telling the truth.' When the judge asked him why he was so sceptical, he replied that none of the five occupants of the car was dressed smartly or was wearing a black tie. The judge asked what they were wearing. 'They were all wearing Manchester United football scarves,' PC Burgess answered. 'And I know for a fact that Manchester United were playing at home that afternoon.'

D Lee Bragg later admitted in court that he didn't really expect to get away with it and that his grandfather, Fred Bragg, wasn't dead. On the contrary, he was fit and well. He also admitted that Fred was a keen Manchester United fan and far from being at his own funeral he was in fact at Manchester United's Old Trafford Stadium that afternoon watching the match. Lee Bragg was fined £65 for speeding, and, to make matters far worse for him, Manchester United lost the match 3–1.

2 Read the text again and answer the questions.
1. Why did the police officer stop Lee Bragg's car?
2. What explanation did Lee Bragg give the police officer?
3. Why were they really late?
4. Why did the policeman think they were lying?
5. Who was Fred Bragg?
6. What did he have in common with his grandson?

3 Find the opposites of these words in the text.
Paragraph A 1 quiet
Paragraph B 2 slightly
           3 to end
Paragraph C 4 believing
Paragraph D 5 denied
           6 better

4 Explain the meaning of the phrases.
1. heavy traffic
2. he knew for a fact
3. on the contrary
4. to make matters far worse

5 Discuss the questions.
1. Have you ever made an excuse to try to get away with something? What was your excuse? What happened in the end?
2. Would you make an excuse in order to see a football match? Which teams would you watch?

80 Unit 9

GRAMMAR

REPORTED SPEECH: QUESTIONS AND COMMANDS

1 Read the examples and answer the questions.

Direct question	Reported question
What **is your name**?	He asked what **his name was**.
Are you in a hurry?	He asked if **he was** in a hurry.

Direct command	Reported command
Get out of your car.	He told him **to get out** of his car.
Don't break the speed limit.	He told him **not to break** the speed limit.

1 Does the verb come before or after the subject in reported questions?
2 In *Yes / No* questions, what word do we usually use in the reported question?
3 In reported commands, what reporting verb do we usually use?
4 What form does the other verb have in reported commands?

2 Rewrite the sentences. Use reported questions.

'What's your name?'
He asked him what his name was.

1 'How do you spell it?'
2 'Do you live in Manchester?'
3 'Is it your car?'
4 'Why were you driving so fast?'
5 'How long have you had your driver's licence?'
6 'When did your grandfather die?'

3 Rewrite the sentences. Use reported commands.

'Get out of the car.'
He told him to get out of the car.

1 'Show me your driver's licence.'
2 'Write down your address.'
3 'Don't tell me any more lies.'
4 'Tell me the truth.'
5 'Don't drive so fast.'
6 'Drive more carefully in future.'

REPORTED SPEECH: SUGGESTIONS

4 Read the sentences and answer the questions.

Direct suggestion	Reported suggestion
'Why don't we **come** to the police station later?'	He suggested that they **came** to the police station later.
'Shall we **go**?'	He suggested that they **went**.

1 How do the verbs change in reported suggestions?
2 What word do we use to start a reported suggestion?

5 Read the dialogue. Then complete the reported speech.

Backpacker   Excuse me. Can you tell me where the station is?
First man   I'm afraid I don't know. Why don't you ask that woman?

The backpacker asked a man *where* the station (1) _____ . The man (2) _____ that she asked a woman.

Backpacker   Excuse me. Which is the best way of getting to the station?
Woman   If I were you, I'd take a taxi or a bus.
Backpacker   I can't afford a taxi, so which bus should I take?
Woman   I'm not sure. I suggest you ask that woman in the kiosk. She knows everything about the buses.

The backpacker then asked a woman. The woman suggested (3) _____ she (4) _____ a bus or a taxi. The backpacker told (5) _____ that she couldn't afford a taxi, and then asked her which bus he should (6) _____ . The woman (7) _____ that she asked the woman in the kiosk.

Backpacker   Excuse me. Which bus goes to the station?
Woman 2   The station? I don't know. Why don't you walk?
Backpacker   That's very helpful. Thanks a lot.

The backpacker asked her which bus (8) _____ to the station. She (9) _____ that she didn't know. She suggested (10) _____ she (11) _____ .

Grammar reference page 109

Unit 9   **81**

Vocabulary

ADVERBS OF MANNER

1 Read the sentences and complete the table.
  a Drive more **slowly**.
  b They drove **well**.

Adjective	Adverb of manner
slow	slowly
nervous	_____
sudden	_____
angry	_____
comfortable	_____
careful	_____
good	_____
hard	_____
fast	_____

2 Complete the text. Use adjectives or adverbs of manner from Exercise 1.

'Now, I know this is your first lesson but don't be *nervous*. Are you sitting (1) _____? Good, now look (2) _____ in both directions before you join the main road. Now drive along this road. Don't drive so (3) _____!'

'The speed limit's 60 kph and you must try (4) _____ to stay below it. Now be (5) _____, there are traffic lights ahead.'

'Wow! I know the lights were red but there was no need to stop so (6) _____!'

'Don't worry. I'm not (7) _____ with you.'

Half an hour later …

That was (8) _____ – congratulations! You drove very '(9) _____ for a first lesson.'

3 Discuss the questions.
  1 Do you ever get nervous? When?
  2 What do you do if you suddenly hear a loud noise?
  3 When you are in a car, do you feel more comfortable when someone is driving fast or slowly?
  4 If one of your friends breaks something of yours, do you shout at them angrily or are you able to control your feelings well?
  5 Do you prefer to do your work slowly and well, or do you prefer to work fast so that you finish earlier?

LISTENING

4 Listen and answer the questions.
  1 In which city does the conversation take place?
  2 What are the four ways of getting to the city centre from the airport?

5 Listen again and answer the questions.
  1 How far is it from the airport to the centre of the city?
  2 What do taxi drivers sometimes do to foreign visitors?
  3 How often do Heathrow Express trains leave?
  4 Where does the Airbus stop on the way to London?
  5 What is another name for the underground?
  6 How long can you use a Travelcard for?

SPEAKING

6 Work in pairs, A and B. A wants information about travelling around your country. B works at a tourist information office. Act out the dialogue.

Student A
Ask about:
• where to visit
• where to stay
• which form of transport to take. (Which is the cheapest, the most comfortable, the fastest / slowest?)

Student B
Prepare answers and tell 'A' what to be careful about. Use phrases like:
If I were you …
You could …
Why don't you …
I suggest …

82   Unit 9

Writing

Checking for accuracy

1 Read the text and find nine mistakes: three spelling mistakes, three punctuation mistakes and three grammar mistakes.

I met my american girlfriend last year when she came to Italy for a holiday. After she left I desperately wanted to see her again, but the main problem was that I lived in Rome and she lived in New York. Luckily my parents very generously offered to lend me the money, so I immediate booked a flight. I didn't tell Laura I was coming. I wanted to surprise her.

The flight to New York took seven hours. I tried hardly to sleep but I couldn't, so the time passed slowly. I got off the plane and took a bus into Manhattan. It was only six in the evening but my body clock kept tell me it was one 'o clock in the morning. I looked nervously around me. Suddenly a man grabbed one of my bags and ran off with it. I was very angry but I wasn't too worried because I still had my passport and my money in my pocket. Then I suddenly remembered that Lauras adress and telephone number were in my bag! I looked in the New York telephone book and tryed to find her number. Unfortunately, Lauras surname is Cohen and there are over 10,000 Cohens in New York!

I flew back to Rome the next day. I never saw Laura again.

2 Correct the mistakes.

	Spelling	Punctuation	Grammar
1	_____	_____	_____
2	_____	_____	_____
3	_____	_____	_____

3 You are going to write a story about a difficult or disastrous journey. It can be real or imaginary. Answer the questions below.

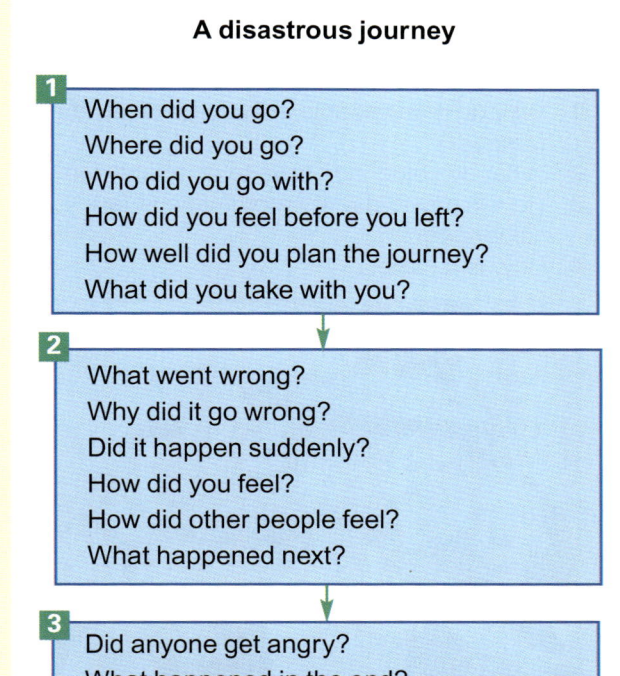

A disastrous journey

1
- When did you go?
- Where did you go?
- Who did you go with?
- How did you feel before you left?
- How well did you plan the journey?
- What did you take with you?

2
- What went wrong?
- Why did it go wrong?
- Did it happen suddenly?
- How did you feel?
- How did other people feel?
- What happened next?

3
- Did anyone get angry?
- What happened in the end?

4 Plan your story. Use your answers to the questions in Exercise 3 to help you. Organize your answers into three paragraphs.

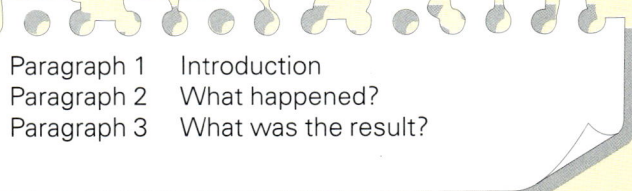

Paragraph 1   Introduction
Paragraph 2   What happened?
Paragraph 3   What was the result?

5 Write a story of about 120–150 words with the title *A disastrous journey*. Use phrasal verbs, adverbs of manner and reported speech if possible. Check your story for spelling, punctuation and grammar mistakes.

Unit 9   83

10 Fame

INTRODUCTION

1 Discuss the questions.
1 Why do many people want to be rich and famous?
2 What do celebrities have to do to stay famous?
3 How is day-to-day life more difficult for celebrities?
4 How is it easier?

READING

2 Read the text. Which of your ideas from Exercise 1 are mentioned? Find ways that day-to-day life is easier or more difficult for celebrities.

3 Read the text again. Are the sentences true or false? Give reasons for your answers.
1 In the *Big Brother* show, the TV audience decided who should leave the house.
2 The writer believes that celebrities worry about money.
3 Celebrities sometimes have problems with their fans.
4 It's difficult for celebrities to have true friends.
5 Geri Bevan already has a boyfriend.
6 According to the text, famous people have an easy life.

4 Find words in the text which match the definitions.
Paragraph A
1 people who watch television
Paragraph B
2 piece of paper that shows how much money you must pay for something
Paragraph C
3 disadvantages
4 someone who is paid to protect a celebrity
5 to have confidence in someone

5 Explain the meaning of the phrases.
1 get into the papers (line 13)
2 at the end of the day (line 48)

DISCUSSION

6 Discuss the questions.
1 Would you like to be a celebrity? Why / Why not?
2 If you were a celebrity, what would you like to be famous for? Why?

84 Unit 10

Public property

A In the TV reality show *Big Brother*, ten ordinary, everyday people were locked in a house for ten weeks and filmed for 24 hours a day. Millions of viewers watched the show, and at the end of each week they decided which contestant should leave. The last person left in the house won £70,000, but all of the contestants became national celebrities.

B Nowadays everyone wants to be famous, and appearing on a TV reality show is a quick way of getting into the papers. But why do we desire fame so much? Put simply, the life of a celebrity looks glamorous and easy. Lifestyle magazines often interview superstars who live in a dream world of chauffeurs, yachts and parties. They can act, play a sport or sing, but they don't have to do much else. They earn lots of money, so they can buy expensive clothes, cars and houses. They don't have to worry about paying bills, and they can go anywhere they want to and travel there first class.

C But what does it really mean to be famous? Are there any drawbacks? As a celebrity, you would be public property. Photographers could take your photo without your permission. Reporters might invent stories about your private life and fans would be constantly asking you for your autograph. You'd have to get bodyguards to protect you and buy security cameras to protect your home. People may want to be your friend, but why? Is it because you're famous or because they really like you? 'I don't trust people now,' says teen popstar Geri Bevan. 'I'd love to have a boyfriend, but it's hard to find someone interested in the real me.'

D Most people think that being rich and famous must be great, but perhaps they should think again. You might be on the cover of a magazine, and there may be lots of people who say they are your friends, but at the end of the day being famous could be a lonely experience.

Unit 10   85

GRAMMAR

MODALS: ABILITY

1 Read the sentences and complete the rules. Use *the future*, *the present*, and *the past*.

a Many celebrities **can** act, play a sport or sing.
b Next year, Matt **will be able to** start theatre school.
c When I was younger, I **could** play the drums.

> 1 We use *can* to talk about ability in _____.
> 2 We use *will be able to* to talk about ability in _____.
> 3 We use *could* to talk about ability in _____.

2 Complete the sentences. Use the correct form of the modals in Exercise 1.

1 Ross _____ write songs when he joined the group, but he can now.
2 Geri _____ act, but she can sing.
3 If you listen to the song carefully, you _____ understand the words.
4 When she was 11, Tina _____ dance very well.
5 The band _____ play well if they don't practise.
6 I _____ play volleyball when I was younger, but I can't now.

3 Read the text about an unusual star. Make five more sentences using *can*, *could* and *will be able to*. Use the numbers in the text to help you.

1 *When he was two, he could ride a bike.*

Charlie is a star with a difference. He was discovered by a film director who saw him (1) riding a bike in a circus when he was only two years old. The director took him to Hollywood where he started acting in films. By the time he was three years old (2) he'd learnt to act and had made his first film. Today, Charlie lives in Beverly Hills and (3) he is still making films. Although he's quite old, (4) he still rides his bike and sometimes he acts. Next year he's stopping work so he'll have more time for his favourite pastimes – (5) climbing trees and (6) eating bananas!

MODALS: OBLIGATION, ADVICE AND PROHIBITION

4 Read the sentences and match the modals with the meanings.

a Celebrities **don't have to** worry about bills.
b Geri **has to** record a new album.
c Jason **must** read the script before his audition.
d You **mustn't** smoke in the cinema.
e You **ought to** do plenty of exercise, even if you are busy.
f You **shouldn't** spend too much money on new clothes.

1 obligation
2 no obligation
3 advice
4 prohibition

> **NOTE!**
> Note that *have to* and *must* have similar meanings, but *don't have to* and *mustn't* have very different meanings.

5 Choose the correct alternative.

1 Fans usually *have to / should* wait for hours if they want a star's autograph.
2 The film audition is tomorrow morning at eight o'clock so Brad *must / should* get up early.
3 I think Paul *ought to / has to* send his songs to a record company. They'd like them.
4 You *mustn't / don't have to* arrive early for the concert. You've already got a seat.
5 You *mustn't / don't have to* make any noise in the recording studio!
6 If you want a record contract, you *should / don't have to* practise more.

6 Discuss the jobs. Use *have to*, *don't have to*, and *should*.

> footballer   TV presenter   opera singer   model
> film director   chef

footballer   *He has to play for a team. He has to be fit. He should train every day. He doesn't have to be good-looking.*

Grammar reference page 110

VOCABULARY

MONEY

1 Complete the sentences. Use the correct form of the verbs in the box.

> ~~waste~~ cost earn run out of spend owe
> give away borrow lend charge afford

You don't need to buy another pair of trainers! Why do you always *waste* your money?

1. The concert was expensive. They _____ me €50 to get in!
2. When Susie first started singing, she didn't _____ much money.
3. Tom only _____ his money on himself. He's very mean.
4. 'I've forgotten my purse. Can I _____ €5?'
5. 'Don't _____ Karl any money. He'll never pay you back!'
6. How much does it _____ to make a record?
7. I wish I could go to the concert, but I can't _____ a ticket.
8. The millionaire was very generous. He _____ a lot of money to help poor people.
9. I can't pay for a taxi home. I've _____ cash!
10. Amy crashed her car. Her parents paid for the repairs, so she _____ them €300.

2 Complete the table. Which verbs are irregular?

VERB	PAST SIMPLE	PAST PARTICIPLE
borrow	*borrowed*	*borrowed*
waste	_____	_____
earn	_____	_____
owe	_____	_____
charge	_____	_____
give away	_____	_____
lend	_____	_____
spend	_____	_____
cost	_____	_____
run out of	_____	_____
afford	_____	_____

3 Answer the questions.
1. What do you spend most of your money on?
2. Do you ever borrow money from your friends?
3. When was the last time you gave away something?
4. Do you think pop stars earn too much money?
5. Have you ever bought anything that was a waste of money?

TALKING ABOUT PRICES

4 Complete the table with the adjectives.

> very cheap   pricey   reasonable   good value

0 € ⬇ €€€€€	free _____ _____ _____ _____ extremely expensive

5 How much are these things in your country? Use the adjectives from Exercise 1.

a video *pricey*

1. a CD
2. a hamburger
3. a pair of designer jeans
4. a teen magazine
5. a cinema ticket
6. a mobile phone

Unit 10 87

READING

1 Look at the title and pictures. Who are the Stones?

Drummer who said 'no' to the Stones

Carlo Little has a stall outside Wembley Stadium. There's a big concert inside and he can hear the fans screaming as the rock band start to play. He flips a burger and thinks to himself 'That could have been me.'

In 1960 Carlo Little was a respected drummer who used to play professionally for a jazz band. Then, two years later, he started playing with a new group called *The Rolling Stones*. 'People were always asking me "Why are you playing with them?"' he remembers. 'They saw me, a professional drummer, playing with young musicians who, at that time, didn't really know what they were doing.' So when the Stones asked him to play with them permanently, he turned them down and went back to his old band.

Since then, he has only seen *The Rolling Stones* once at a concert in London. After the show, he went backstage. It must have been a difficult moment for Carlo and in the end he was too embarrassed to say hello. Instead he walked out, and he has not been in contact with the band members since then.

Today he often reflects on the past and how things might have been different. He could have had millions of fans, gone on world tours and lived in a huge mansion. But instead he became a telephone engineer, and then a greengrocer. Eventually Carlo spent 15 years as a bread salesman, getting up in the early hours to drive a bakery van.

'I'm quite sorry about it all,' he admits, 'because I know I was a good drummer. I often think about what might have happened. But things could be worse,' he adds with a smile. 'I've got a nice life and I'm alive and well. I'm happy with my life.'

2 Read the text. What mistake did Carlo make?

3 Read the text again. For questions 1–6, choose the correct answer A, B, or C.

1. What is Carlo doing at Wembley Stadium?
   A Watching a concert.
   B Playing in a concert.
   C Cooking food.
2. Why did Carlo leave the Stones?
   A They didn't want him.
   B People didn't think they were a good band.
   C He wanted to form his own band.
3. When he left the Stones, Carlo
   A went on tour.
   B joined his old band.
   C worked as a greengrocer.
4. When Carlo saw the Stones backstage he
   A offered to play for them.
   B said hello.
   C didn't say anything.
5. If Carlo had stayed with the Stones he
   A wouldn't have had many fans.
   B would have seen the world.
   C wouldn't have earned much money.
6. When Carlo thinks about the Stones he
   A regrets his decision.
   B is happy he turned them down.
   C feels angry because he was a good drummer.

4 Match the words from the text with the definitions.

1	respected (line 10)	a	a highly-trained person who is paid for his / her work
2	a professional (line 17)	b	in the end
3	turned down (line 20)	c	admired
4	backstage (line 22)	d	thinks about
5	reflects on (line 27)	e	said no
6	eventually (line 31)	f	part of a concert hall where bands wait to go on

5 Discuss the questions.

1. How did becoming rich affect Carlo's friendship with the Stones?
2. If you were Carlo and you met the Stones, how would you feel?
3. Have you ever lost contact with someone, and then regretted it afterwards?

88 Unit 10

GRAMMAR

MODALS: POSSIBILITY AND CERTAINTY

1 Read the sentences and complete the rules. Use *may*, *might*, *can't* and *must*.
  a Carlo **may** be at work or he **could** be at home.
  b We **might** go to the Rolling Stones concert.
  c Carlo worked late last night. He **must** be tired.
  d Carlo sells hamburgers. He **can't** be very happy.

> 1 We use _____ to say that we are certain that something is true.
> 2 We use *could*, _____ and _____ to say that something is possible.
> 3 We use _____ to say that we are sure something isn't true.

2 Complete the sentences. Use the modals in brackets.

  Perhaps Carlo will sell a lot of hamburgers. (may)
  Carlo may sell a lot of hamburgers.
  1 It's possible that the concert will be on TV. (might)
    The concert …
  2 Maybe Carlo will retire next year. (could)
    Carlo …
  3 It's likely that he'll give up playing the drums. (could)
    He …
  4 We don't know if we'll call our band *Rain*. (might)
    We …
  5 There's a possibility that the radio station won't play our record. (may)
    The …

3 Complete the sentences. Use *can't* or *must* and the verb in brackets.

  Brett has got hundreds of CDs. He (know) *must know* a lot about music.
  1 The group has sold millions of records. They (be) _____ very good.
  2 Jemma (sing) _____ in the band! She's got a terrible voice.
  3 You (feel) _____ tired. You've been practising all day.
  4 Carlo (regret) _____ his decision. I don't believe he's happy.
  5 The concert (be) _____ cancelled. Lots of people are already there.

MODALS + PERFECT INFINITIVE

4 Read the sentences and match rules 1–3 with a–c.
He **can't have earned** much money.
Carlo **must have felt** embarrassed when he saw the band.
He **could have lived** in a mansion.

> 1 We use *must* + *have* + past participle
> 2 We use *could*, *may*, *might* + *have* + past participle
> 3 We use *can't* + *have* + past participle
>
> a to say that something is possible in the past.
> b to say that something is impossible in the past.
> c to say that we are certain that something is true in the past.

5 Complete the sentences. Use modals and *have* + past participle.

  The group has sold millions of records. They (must / earn) *must have earned* a lot of money.
  1 I can't find my mobile phone. I (must / leave) _____ it in the studio.
  2 The manager was disappointed with the group. They (could / play) _____ better.
  3 People left before the end of the concert. It (can't / be) _____ very good.
  4 The lead singer left the band. He (may / have) _____ an argument.
  5 The Stones ignored Carlo. They (might not / recognize) _____ him.

6 Write sentences about the pictures. Use modals and *have* + past participle.

  she / win / award
  She might have won an award.

  1 the concert / finish

  2 he / forget / his lines

  3 he / hurt / himself

Grammar reference page 110

Unit 10

VOCABULARY

PHRASAL VERBS: THE MUSIC INDUSTRY

1 Match the phrasal verbs with the definitions.
1. Tickets for the Britney Spears concert **sold out** in less than an hour.
2. The group **split up** after an argument about money.
3. The record company **signed up** the rap singer for two albums.
4. Rachel decided to **take up** the drums. She wanted to start her own rock group.
5. The singer **turned down** the record contract. They hadn't offered her enough money.
6. Although they argued a lot, the group decided to **keep on** playing together.

a begin to do something
b refused something
c continue to do something
d get someone to sign a contract and work for you
e all bought, with nothing left
f stopped playing together

2 Discuss the questions.
1. Have you ever been to a pop concert?
2. What was the last concert you went to or watched on TV?
3. Who gave the concert? Was it sold out?
4. Did you enjoy it? Why / Why not?

LISTENING

3 Listen to the interview and answer the questions.

1. Is the Pop Star Academy easy to get into?
2. Do you have to do a lot of auditions?

4 Listen again. For questions 1–4, choose the correct answer A, B, or C.
1. How many people apply to the Academy each year?
   A thousands
   B 20,000
   C hundreds   [1]
2. How many people take part in each audition?
   A two
   B ten
   C twenty   [2]
3. For your audition, you should choose a song
   A which you like.
   B which is new.
   C which is famous.   [3]
4. The most important way the Academy helps you is by
   A preparing you for the downside.
   B giving you advice about the music industry.
   C increasing your confidence.   [4]

PRONUNCIATION

5 Listen and repeat. Pay special attention to the /ɔː/ sound in the sentences.
1. I <u>ough</u>t to say …
2. My first <u>au</u>dition …
3. <u>Your</u> sc<u>ore</u> was very p<u>oor</u>.
4. He <u>al</u>ways has <u>aw</u>ful <u>au</u>ditions.
5. She <u>or</u>dered the <u>au</u>thor to sign <u>au</u>tographs in <u>Au</u>gust.

SPEAKING

6 Imagine you are a journalist interviewing someone from the Popstar Academy. Complete the questions.
1. What instrument / you play?
2. What type of music / you like?
3. you / write / your own songs?
4. How / you feel / during the audition?
5. record company / sign you up yet?

7 Think of three more questions using these phrasal verbs.

> take up   keep on   turn down

8 In pairs, take it in turns to interview each other. Imagine the pop star's answers.

90 Unit 10

Writing

Checking content

1 Read the essays and answer the questions.

Which essay:
1. includes irrelevant information?
2. is divided into logical paragraphs?
3. uses expressions to order ideas?

A

<u>What are the arguments for and against winning the lottery?</u>

Most of us dream about winning the lottery and becoming famous. However, although it may appear to be a dream come true, winning the lottery can sometimes be a negative experience.

Lottery winners have many advantages. Firstly, they have enough money to realise their personal dreams. Secondly, they have the power to change people's lives. They can give their money to family and friends, or make donations to charities.

However, there are disadvantages. It could be difficult to decide how to spend your money, and you may argue with your family or lose your friends. Some people could be jealous of you, and hundreds of others could send you letters asking for money. In addition, you might not be sure if the 'new' people you meet are real friends or not.

In conclusion, although lottery winners may seem lucky, there are actually many disadvantages. Personally, I wouldn't want to win the lottery.

B

<u>What are the arguments for and against winning the lottery?</u>

Many people want to win the lottery and become famous. That's not surprising because lottery winners have fantastic lives. But are there any disadvantages in winning the lottery? When we read about lottery winners, the first thing we notice is how rich they are. Winners have everything – expensive clothes, sports cars and fantastic houses. They are interviewed by magazines and newspapers, and some appear on television! Everyone wants to meet them and ask them about their story.

I think lottery winners have a great life and the money they win can solve a lot of problems. I can't really think of any disadvantages. When I read about the lucky winners in the newspaper, I often dream about winning the lottery myself! Unfortunately I can't buy lottery tickets as my parents think they're a waste of money. But I'd like to buy a ticket someday, and I still think that lottery winners are incredibly lucky people.

2 Look at essay B again. Find sentences that you think a) support winning the lottery, and b) contain irrelevant information. Discuss your ideas.

3 Are there any sentences in essay B that are against winning the lottery?

4 Look at Exercises 1–3 again. How could essay B be improved?

5 You are going to write an essay with the title *'What are the arguments for and against being famous?'*. Plan your essay. Use your answers to the questions to help you.
1. What would you do with the money you earned?
2. How often could you see your family?
3. Would you trust your friends?
4. Would you need a bodyguard?
5. Could you use your fame to help people?
6. How would you feel if reporters followed you everywhere?

6 Write a draft of your essay of about 120–150 words. Use the paragraph plan below to help you.

Paragraph 1: Introduction to the topic and your opinion.
Paragraph 2: Arguments for being famous.
Paragraph 3: Arguments against being famous.
Paragraph 4: Conclusion and summing up your opinion.

7 Check your essay. Make sure that:
- you have answered the question. Don't include irrelevant information.
- your ideas are ordered into logical paragraphs – introduction, main arguments, conclusion.

8 Write your essay again. Include the changes you made in Exercise 7.

Unit 10 91

Units 9–10: revision

GRAMMAR

REPORTED SPEECH

1 Read the dialogue and the reported conversation. Choose the correct alternative.

Kelly How much are the tickets for the Britney Spears concert?
Neil They're £30.
Kelly What time does the concert start?
Neil At 8 o'clock. Have you been to one of her concerts before?
Kelly No, I haven't.
Neil How are you going to pay?
Kelly I'll use my credit card.

Kelly asked Neil how much (1) *were the tickets / the tickets were* for the Britney Spears' concert. Neil told her they (2) *were / are* £30. Kelly asked him what time (3) *did the concert start / the concert started*. Neil said it started at 8 o'clock. He then asked her if she (4) *have been / had been* to one of Britney Spears' concerts before. Kelly replied that she (5) *didn't / hadn't*. He then asked her how (6) *was she going to / she was going to* pay. Kelly explained that she (7) *would / will* use her credit card.

2 Rewrite the dialogue in reported speech.

1 Police officer What's your name?
   He asked me *what my name was*.
2 Lee Lee Jarvis.
   I said that …
3 Police officer Show me your driver's licence, please Mr Jarvis.
   He told …
4 Lee I haven't got it with me.
   I explained that …
5 Police officer OK, bring it to the police station tomorrow.
   He told me …
6 Lee All right, I will. Can I go now?
   I agreed and then asked him …
7 Police officer Yes, you can. But don't forget to bring in your licence.
   He agreed but told me …

MODALS

3 Read the text and choose the correct alternative.

Matt Hanson organizes tours for some of the world's biggest bands. But what does it take to be a tour organizer?

'People think organizing tours (1) *must be / can't be* a great job. But a band (2) *must be / might be* months on tour, and it's a pretty exhausting schedule. Some tours (3) *may / must* visit more than 20 towns and cities, and for each concert we (4) *can / have to* set up the stage, and check the sound and lighting. In addition, some concerts (5) *might / should* involve hundreds of people and lots of equipment, and tours (6) *can't / may* need up to twenty lorries just to carry everything.

As a tour organizer you (7) *may / should* make sure you get plenty of sleep before the tour. Once the tour starts you (8) *have to / could* make sure everything goes smoothly. If the support band doesn't turn up you (9) *don't have to / mustn't* panic! The most important part of the job is to solve problems quickly.

I think the best thing about being on tour is the last concert. After that I (10) *can / might* relax and go home – I (11) *mustn't / don't have to* worry about the next show.

4 Complete the sentences with the correct form of the verbs in brackets.

There's no one at the concert. They (can't / advertise) *can't have advertised* it.
1 The band were disappointed after the concert. It (could / be) _____ better.
2 Lee looks very tired. He (must / finish) _____ work late last night.
3 Brett knows the words to the song. He (might / hear) _____ it on the radio.
4 The support band haven't arrived yet. They (could / have) _____ an accident.
5 Paul got to the bus stop a bit late. He (could / miss) _____ the bus.
6 The concert sold out weeks ago. Lucy (can't / buy) _____ tickets last night.
7 I've lost my purse. I (might / leave) _____ at the café.

Vocabulary

Phrasal verbs

1 Complete the dialogue using the correct form of the phrasal verbs in the box.

> get out   get away with   get away from   get back
> get on   get by   get over   get somebody down
> get away

Kris Well, it's a beautiful island and you always said you liked to (1) _____ all your fans sometimes.

Dani Yes, I needed to (2) _____ of Los Angeles. All those photographers were beginning to (3) _____.

Kris What did you tell your manager?

Dani I told him I had to work on my new album. He was worried at first but later he (4) _____ it. Of course I didn't tell him I was just going away on holiday. But I think I (5) _____ it. And even if he found out, I don't think he'd mind, because we (6) _____ very well. In fact we're good friends, and he knows how much I've wanted to (7) _____ and be on my own for a bit.

Kris But when are you going to (8) _____ to work?

Dani Maybe in a month. I'm not sure yet. Everybody will just have to (9) _____ without me for a change. Right now I

2 Complete the sentences. Use the correct form of the phrasal verbs in the box.

> sell out   set out   sign up   break down   take up
> hold up   turn down   keep on

1. The bus _____ on the way to school. We had to wait an hour for the next one.
2. The tour was a huge success. Each concert _____ months in advance.
3. A traffic jam _____ us _____. That's why we're late.
4. After the audition, the record company were so impressed that they _____ the band.
5. Karl _____ the electric guitar instead of the violin. He wanted to be a pop star.
6. Pete _____ the offer to go on a world tour. He was too busy.
7. During the concert some fans got onto the stage, but the group _____ playing.
8. We _____ early in the morning because we wanted to avoid the traffic.

Adverbs of manner

3 Complete the sentences with adjectives or adverbs of manner formed from the words in the box.

> angry   slow   fast   good   comfortable   sudden
> careful   nervous   hard

1. He drove so _____ that there was always a queue of cars behind him.
2. She'd never flown before so she was quite _____ although she tried _____ not to show it.
3. Before I left I checked very _____ that I'd got my passport and my tickets.
4. The seats on the plane were very _____, so Dave slept _____ during the flight.
5. The taxi driver drove quite _____ so Emma arrived in plenty of time for her meeting.
6. The driver of the car behind me was very _____ because I stopped very _____ and he nearly drove into the back of me.

Money

4 Complete the text with verbs about money.

> Pop stars don't *earn* a lot of money when they go on tour. The average band (1) _s____ thousands of pounds on concerts, and they often have to (2) _b____ money to pay for equipment and stage sets. In fact new pop bands often can't (3) _a____ to go on tour because tours (4) _c____ a huge amount of money to organize.
>
> Fans may complain when they are (5) _c____ €40 or €50 for a ticket, but the truth is that many pop bands get into debt and (6) _o____ money to the bank at the end of a tour. Some bands even (7) _r____ o____ o____ money and have to cancel concerts. So why do pop bands (8) _w____ their money on tours? The answer is publicity. Having good publicity helps them to get new fans and sell more CDs.

5 Complete the sentences.

1. When I'm older I want to earn …
2. The last time I lent someone money …
3. I wish I could afford …
4. I'd like to give away …
5. It's a waste of money to …

> Now look at the song on page 98.

Revision 9–10   93

Songbook: Units 1–2

1 Read the information about Otis Redding and answer the questions.

1. Where did Otis write his most successful song?
2. Why did he have to leave school?
3. In what ways did he earn money?
4. How did he get his first record contract?
5. What was his ambition?

FACTFILE: OTIS REDDING

Otis Redding was staying in a houseboat, looking out across San Francisco Bay, when he wrote *Sittin' on the dock of the bay*. The song became his biggest worldwide hit, but it was also his last. Just days after the recording Otis was killed in a plane crash. He was only 26 years old.

Otis was born in Georgia in 1941 and began his musical career in a church choir. Times were hard for the Redding family, so Otis dropped out of school early and started working in bands. He also entered talent shows for $5 cash prizes, and won fifteen in a row!

Then in 1962 Otis got his big break. He was working at a recording studio in Memphis when he was offered the chance to record his own songs. The result was so good that studio executives offered him a contract.

Otis became one of the most influential American soul singers of the 1960s. He wanted his music to bring together different races and cultures and, in his short life, he achieved his ambition. Today his songs, with their timeless and universal lyrics, are still popular with audiences all over the world.

2 Listen and complete the song.

(Sittin' On) The Dock of the Bay

Sittin' in the (1) ____ sun,
I'll be sittin' when the evening comes,
Watching the (2) ____ roll in,
And then I'll watch 'em roll away again, yeah,
I'm sittin' on the dock of the bay,
Watching the tide roll away,
I'm just sittin' on the dock of the bay,
Wasting time.

I left my (3) ____ in Georgia,
Headed for the 'Frisco bay
'Cause I have (4) ____ to live for,
And looks like nothing's gonna come my way,

So I'm just gonna sit on the dock of the bay
Watching the tide roll away,
I'm sittin' on the dock of the bay,
Wasting time.

Look like nothing's gonna (5) ____
Everything still remains the same,
I can't do what ten (6) ____ tell me to do,
So I guess I'll remain the same, yeah.

Sittin' here resting my (7) ____,
And this loneliness won't leave me alone, yes,
It's two (8) ____ miles I roamed
Just to make this dock my home

Now I'm just gonna sit at the dock of the bay
Watching the tide roll away,
Sittin' on the dock of the bay,
Wasting time.

gonna = going to
'Cause = because

3 Match the words and phrases with the definitions.

1 headed for   a go well for you
2 come my way   b travelled towards
3 remain the same   c travel with no fixed destination
4 roam   d never change

4 Answer the questions.

1. The song is about someone who:
   A has lost his job.
   B is not sure what to do and misses his home.
   C has split up with his girlfriend.
   D is travelling round the world.

2. Which adjectives describe the singer?

   contented / excited / depressed / anxious / angry / ambitious / determined

5 Discuss the questions.

1. Why is the singer 'wasting time'?
2. What advice would you give him?

Songbook: Units 3–4

1 Read the information about Britney Spears. Are the statements true or false?
1. Britney didn't start singing until she was eight.
2. When her first single came out she had never appeared on TV before.
3. Britney set a new world record with her first single.
4. She has acted in several films.
5. Being famous has completely changed Britney.

FACTFILE: BRITNEY SPEARS

Britney Spears was born on 2 December 1981 in the small town of Kentwood in the south of the USA. She started appearing in talent shows and choirs at an early age, and by the time she was eight she was studying performing arts in New York. There she was spotted by talent scouts and she was soon appearing in television commercials. One thing led to another and at the age of 16 she recorded her first hit single – *Baby one more time*. It went straight to Number 1 all over the world, as did her debut album. Britney was the most successful newcomer in recording history!

Since then she's never looked back. Hits like *(You drive me) crazy* have followed, along with worldwide concert tours. In 2001 she starred in her first movie, *Crossroads*, then she briefly appeared in an Austin Powers movie. Britney has become an all-round entertainer!

Not surprisingly fame has had a big impact on Britney's life – although some things haven't changed. Her favourite food is still hot dogs and ice cream, and her favourite hobbies are shopping, watching movies and driving her go-kart!

2 Listen and complete the song.

3 Explain the meaning of the words and phrases.
1. go my way
2. in between
3. It's time that I …
4. face up to

4 What's the song about? Choose the correct answer.
A a girl's first boyfriend
B a girl's first feelings of independence
C a relationship between a girl and an older woman

I used to think
I had the (1) ____ to everything
But now I know
That (2) ____ doesn't always
Go my way, yeah …

It feels like I'm (3) ____ in the middle
That's when I realized …

Chorus
I'm not a girl
Not yet a woman
All I need is time
A (4) ____ that is mine
While I'm in between.

I'm not a girl
There is no need to (5) ____ me
It's time that I
Learn to face up to this on my own
I've seen so much more than you know now
So don't tell me to (6) ____ my eyes.

Chorus

I'm not a girl
But if you look at me closely
You will see it my (7) ____
This girl will always find
Her way.

I'm not a girl
(I'm not a girl don't tell me what to (8) ____)
Not yet a woman
I'm just trying to find the woman in me, yeah
All I need is time
All I need is (9) ____ that is mine
While I'm in between.

I'm not a girl, not yet a woman

5 Discuss the questions.
1. What does the singer want?
2. Who do you think she is talking to when she says 'There is no need to protect me' and 'don't tell me what to believe'?
3. Do you think she feels confident, afraid or confused? Why?
4. How do you think her parents feel?

Songs 95

Songbook: Units 5–6

1 Read the information about Tina Cousins and complete the sentences.
1. Although Tina was a model, she …
2. Tina first sang at a fashion show because …
3. She got a contract with a top record producer but …
4. Sash contacted Tina because …
5. When the hurricane hit Puerto Rico, Tina …

FACTFILE:
TINA COUSINS

Tina Cousins comes from Essex, near London, in England. Because of her looks she started working as a fashion model, but she always knew that she had a good singing voice.

Her breakthrough came at a big fashion show when the singer didn't arrive and Tina volunteered to replace her. People were surprised by her talent and afterwards she was signed up by a top record producer. The resulting record, *Killin' Time*, didn't do too well, but a German DJ called Sash heard it. He was fascinated by her voice, so he contacted Tina and together they made a single called *Mysterious Times*, which was a huge hit.

Since then Tina has performed in many different countries. It's a glamorous career, but it's also had its scary moments. Once when she was in Puerto Rico a hurricane hit the island. 'We had to rush to the airport to get the last plane out,' says Tina. 'There were people crying in the departure lounge. It was awful.'

But the experience hasn't stopped Tina from flying, and, fortunately for her fans, she'll still be touring all over the world in the future!

2 Listen and complete the song.

Nothing to Fear

Come to me and I'll light your darkness
Oh baby, can't you see
That I can make you shine
So breathe me (1) _____ and I'll make you conscious
'Cause I can give you peace and I can make it right
So close your eyes (2) _____ will be alright
Nothing to fear as long as I'm here
Close your eyes now.

Close your eyes and (3) _____ me around you
And baby let me show that I'm all you need to know
Just ease your mind there's nothing to fear now
'Cause I can give you (4) _____ and I can make it grow.

So close your eyes everything will be alright
Nothing to fear as long as I'm here
Close your eyes now.

Let me show you love can be (5) _____
Let me show you love can be wonderful
I know you have a wounded (6) _____
But I can make it heal
And I will (7) _____ turn away because my love is real.

So close your eyes everything will be alright
Nothing to fear as long as I'm here
Close your eyes now.

3 Complete the table. Find words in the song which rhyme with these words.

1	light	right	_____
2	show	_____	_____
3	dear	_____	_____
4	feel	_____	_____

4 Explain the meaning of the words and phrases.
1. light your darkness
2. ease your mind
3. wounded
4. turn away

5 Discuss the questions.
1. Who do you think Tina is singing to? How does that person feel?
2. What do you think has happened to the person?
3. What does Tina promise in the song?
4. Why does she ask him / her to close their eyes?

Songbook: Units 7–8

1 Read the information about Avril Lavigne and put the events in order.

a Avril finished recording an album.
b She met a good producer.
c She gave concerts in different cities.
d She decided to be a singer.
e She started work on her own songs.
f She lived in New York.

FACTFILE: AVRIL LAVIGNE

Avril Lavigne is often described as 'anything but ordinary'. Others describe her as 'outrageous'. She comes from the small Canadian town of Napanee.

Avril was just a kid when she made up her mind about what she wanted to do. She wanted to sing. To start with she sang in her bedroom. Then, as she got older, she sang wherever she could. Before long someone from Arista Records spotted her. She was only 16 at the time, but she left school and went to Manhattan.

In Manhattan she started writing songs for her first album and virtually lived in the recording studio. But things didn't work out and the album wasn't finished, so she went to Los Angeles to make a fresh start. It was good move. If she'd stayed in New York, she might never have met Cliff Magnes. Cliff was a songwriter / producer and completely understood what Avril was about. The result was the album *Let Go* followed by a nationwide tour.

Avril goes to great lengths to make her music 'real'. 'I write what I feel,' she says. 'I never worry what others think. I'm going to dress what's me and sing what's me. I want to rock the world.'

2 Listen and complete the song.

3 Match the phrases with the meanings.

1 stuck up their nose
2 her head was up in space
3 tags along
4 missed out
5 more than meets the eye

a lost a good opportunity
b thought someone wasn't as good as them
c not judge people by their appearance
d had a high opinion of herself
e follows or goes with someone

sk8ter Boi

He was a boy, she was a girl
Can I make it any more obvious?
He was a punk, she did ballet
What more can I (1) _____,?
He wanted her, she'd never tell
Secretly, she wanted him as (2) _____
But all of her friends, they stuck up their nose
They had a problem with his baggy (3) _____ .

He was a sk8ter boi
She said, 'See ya later boy!'
He wasn't good enough for her
She had a pretty face
But her head was up in (4) _____
She needed to come back down to Earth.

Five years from now, she sits at home
Feeding the baby, she's all (5) _____
She turns on TV, guess who she sees?
Sk8er Boi, rockin' up MTV
She calls up her friends, they already know
And they've all got tickets to see his (6) _____
She tags along, but stands in the crowd
Looks up at the man that she turned down.

He was a sk8ter boi
She said, 'See ya later boy!'
He wasn't good enough for her
Now he's a superstar
Slammin' on his (7) _____
Does your pretty face see what he's worth?

Sorry, girl, but you missed out
Well, tough luck, that boy's mine now
We are more than just good friends
This is how the story (8) _____
Too bad that you couldn't see
See that man the boy could (9) _____
There is more than meets the eye
I see the soul that is inside
He's just a boy and I'm just a girl
Can I make it any more obvious?
We are in love, haven't you heard
How we rock each other's world?

I met the sk8ter boi,
I said, 'See ya later, boy!'
I'll be backstage after the show
I'll be at the studio singing the song we wrote
About a girl he used to (10) _____ .

sk8ter boi = skater boy, or a boy who skateboards

4 Discuss the questions.
1 What mistake did the girl in the song make?
2 Do you think she regrets her mistake? Why / Why not?
3 Is it acceptable to judge people by their appearances?

Songs 97

Songbook: Units 9–10

1 Read the information about 'N SYNC and answer the questions.
1. How did 'N SYNC start?
2. What does their name mean?
3. When did the band record their first song?
4. Why was their third album called *Celebrity*?
5. What does JC think is special about their records?

FACTFILE:
'N SYNC

Things might have been very different if Chris Kirkpatrick hadn't called Justin Timberlake in 1996. Chris told him he had a great idea for a new band, and that idea became a group called 'N SYNC. The name was made up of the last letters of the band member's names: Justin, Chris, Joey, Lansten and JC. It also described what they did – the boys were 'in sync.' or singing and moving in time with each other. In fact they did this so well that a record company soon signed them up, and less than a year later they released their first single. It went straight into the top 10.

Their first album was also an overnight success and sold over 10 million copies. The follow up album *No Strings Attached* sold even better – 2.4 million copies in the first week. Before long they became the music industry's biggest earners. Their next album, *Celebrity*, took a humorous look at fame, making fun of their legendary status in pop music.

According to JC 'You can't really classify our music. Our formula has always been about five people coming together to brainstorm. Each person adds their own flavour and the combination is what defines 'N SYNC.'

2 Listen and complete the song.

Chorus

If I wasn't a celebrity
Would you be so (1) _____ to me?
If I couldn't have Gs like everyday
Would you still wanna be with me?
If I couldn't buy you (2) _____ rings
And all those other expensive things
Would you be so into me?
If I wasn't a celebrity.

(Lately)
I did a little thinking
'Bout the things
That satisfy you
It's making me (3) _____
'Bout the things that
You see in me
(4) _____ the way you
You like to say your
Man's a (5) _____
Baby what's the deal?
I thought you wanted me for me.

Say what you mean
Mean what you say
(6) _____ me away
'Cause I ain't got
No time to play
So I say

Chorus

'Bout = about
ain't = isn't

3 Explain the meaning of the phrases.
1. Would you be so into me?
2. I done a little thinking
3. what's the deal?
4. Say what you mean

4 What is the song about? Choose the correct answer.
A what it's like to be famous.
B how some people want to be famous.
C how some people are only interested in celebrities because they're famous.

5 Discuss the questions.
1. Who do you think the band are talking to? Do they trust them? Why / Why not?
2. What do they mean when they say 'I thought you wanted me for me'?
3. What other difficulties might celebrities face? Think about the texts you read in Unit 10. Did those texts mention any other problems?

Grammar reference

UNIT 1

PRESENT SIMPLE

Affirmative

I	agree
he / she / it	agrees
you / we / they	agree

Negative

I	don't	
he / she / it	doesn't	agree
you / we / they	don't	

Question

do	I	
does	he / she / it	agree?
do	you / we / they	

We use the present simple to talk about
- habits or regular activities.
  I *play* tennis every day.
- facts or things that are always true.
  Water *boils* at 100°C.
  Olympic athletes *train* very hard.

PRESENT CONTINUOUS

Affirmative

I	'm	
he / she / it	's	studying
you / we / they	're	

Negative

I	'm not	
he / she / it	isn't	studying
you / we / they	aren't	

Questions

am	I	
is	he / she / it	studying?
are	you / we / they	

We use the present continuous to talk about
- things that are in progress now.
  He*'s having* breakfast in the kitchen.
- temporary situations.
  We*'re staying* with friends for a week.
- future arrangements.
  We*'re leaving* at 8.30.

STATIVE VERBS

Some verbs are almost never used in the present continuous, present perfect continuous or past continuous tenses. These are known as *stative verbs*. The most common stative verbs are

Verbs of thinking: *understand, know, remember, believe, forget, mean*
I *understand* what you're saying.

Verbs of liking and disliking: *like, love, prefer, hate*
He *doesn't like* spaghetti.

Verbs of being and possession: *be, own, belong, contain*
We *know* what you've been doing.

THE GERUND

We use the gerund
- as the subject of a sentence.
  Smoking is bad for you.
  Shopping can be really boring.
- after prepositions.
  The thought *of going* on holiday was exciting.
  I'm interested *in joining* a tennis club.
- after certain verbs. These include: admit, avoid, can't stand, consider, don't mind, finish, give up, mention, practise, risk, suggest.
  I *can't stand waiting* for buses.
  She *suggested going* to the cinema.

WANT

We use *want + object + infinitive* to talk about what we want other people to do.
I *want you to listen* carefully.
She didn't *want us to leave* the party.

Grammar reference 99

UNIT 2

PAST SIMPLE

Affirmative

| I / he / she / it / we / you / they | worked |

Negative

| I / he / she / it / we / you / they | didn't | work |

Questions

| did | I / he / she / it / we / you / they | work? |

We use the past simple
- to talk about completed events or actions in the past
  I *left* Buenos Aires *in 1998*.
  What time did you *finish* your homework?
- to talk about something that happened regularly in the past.
  They *played* basketball after school *every day*.
  He *went* to French classes *for years*.
- after *when* to talk about past events.
  We walked to school *when* we *lived* in Bursa.
  When did you *leave*?

PAST CONTINUOUS

Affirmative

I	was	
he / she / it	was	eating
we / you / they	were	

Negative

I	wasn't	
he / she / it	wasn't	eating
we / you / they	weren't	

Questions

was	I	
was	he / she / it	eating?
were	we / you / they	

We use the past continuous
- to talk about something that was in progress at a certain time in the past.
  At 12.00 I *was talking* to Hannah on the phone.
- to talk about an interrupted action in the past.
  I *was cooking* my dinner *when* the doorbell rang.
- after *while* or *as* to talk about something that was in progress.
  While I *was walking*, it *started* to rain.
  As he *was leaving*, he *saw* her.

PAST PERFECT SIMPLE

Affirmative

| I / he / she / it / we / you / they | had | finished |

Negative

| I / he / she / it / we / you / they | hadn't | finished |

Questions

| had | I / he / she / it / we / you / they | finished? |

We use the past perfect simple to talk about
- past actions or situations which happened before another past action or situation.
  Susie looked in her bag. She*'d forgotten* her mobile phone!
- events before a specific time in the past.
  By 6.00 we *had washed* the dishes and *cooked* a pizza.

USED TO

Affirmative

| I / he / she / it / you / we / they | used to | live in London |

Negative

| I / he / she / it / you / we / they | didn't use to | live in London |

Questions

| did | I / he / she / it / you / we / they | use to | live in London? |

We use *used to* to talk about a habit, regular activity or situation in the past.
I *used* to cycle to school.
We *didn't use* to have a video recorder.
Where did you *use* to live?

- If we talk about the period of time that a habit, regular activity or state occurred, we have to use the past simple.
  I ~~used to live~~ *lived* in Athens for six years.
  We ~~used to go~~ *went* to that school from 1999–2002.

NOTE!

We can also use *would* to talk about past habits or typical behaviour.
I *would often visit* my grandparents on the way home from school.
I *wouldn't finish* my homework until the last minute before class.

100 Grammar reference

Uses of the past simple, *used to* and *would*

Tense	Uses		
	Past habits	Past states	Single past actions
past simple	I played tennis on Fridays.	I lived in Rome.	We moved to a new flat in 2001.
used to	I used to play tennis on Fridays.	I used to live in Rome.	
would	I would play tennis on Fridays.		

- We can use the past simple, *used to* or *would* to talk about past habits and regular actions.
  I often **went swimming** with Helen.
  We **used to** have parties on the beach in summer.
  She **would** never tell you what she was thinking.

- If we talk about past states, we have to use the past simple or *used to*.
  I ~~would live~~ **lived / used to live** in Birmingham before we moved here.

- If we talk about single past actions, we have to use the past simple.
  I ~~would see~~ **saw** Kylie in concert in 2002.
  I ~~used to have~~ **had** a special party for my sixteenth birthday.

GET USED TO

Tense	Form	
infinitive	to get used to	
present continuous	I'm getting used to	
past simple	I got used to	
past continuous	I was getting used to	
present perfect	I've got used to	
past perfect	I'd got used to	walking to school
will	I'll get used to	
going to	I'm going to get used to	
future continuous	I'll be getting used to	
future perfect	I'll have got used to	

- We use a noun or a gerund (but not an infinitive) after *be / get used to*.
  I'm **used to crowds** of people, because I work in a café.
  I've got **used to** ~~eat~~ **eating** my breakfast quickly in the morning, so I can spend an extra ten minutes in bed.

We use *get used to* when something that was strange is becoming familiar or normal.
They've **got used to** working nights.
He's **getting used to** wearing glasses.

- We don't normally use *get used to* in the present simple tense.
  I ~~get used to~~ **'m getting used to** the terrible weather in England.
  They ~~get used to~~ **are used to** the spicy food here now.

BE USED TO

Tense	Form	
infinitive	to be used to	
present simple	I'm used to	
past simple	I was used to	waking up early
present perfect	I've been used to	
past perfect	I'd been used to	
will	I'll be used to	

We use *be used to* when something isn't strange or unfamiliar any more, but is normal.
She's **used to** driving on the motorway.
We're **used to** having sandwiches for lunch.

- We don't normally use *be used to* in continuous tenses.
  The language was a problem when Tracy first moved to Turkey, but now she ~~is being used to~~ **is used to** speaking Turkish.

UNIT 3

COMPARATIVES AND SUPERLATIVES

Type of adjective	Comparative form	Superlative form	Examples
short words	+ er	+ est	faster, fastest
short words ending in -e	+ r	+ st	larger, largest
short words ending in a vowel and a consonant	double the consonant + er	double the consonant + est	bigger, biggest
words ending in -y	y + ier	y + iest	tidier, tidiest
long words	+ more / less	+ the most / the least	more beautiful, the least beautiful
irregular forms	different word	different word	better, best

- We use comparatives to compare two things. We use superlatives to compare three or more things.
  I'm *taller than* my sister.
  Lucy is the *most intelligent* student in the class.

NOTE!

We can use *less* and *least* with long adjectives. These have the opposite meaning to *more* and *most*.
Physics is the least interesting subject. (the most boring)
Watching TV is less enjoyable than going to concerts. (concerts are more enjoyable)

(NOT) AS + ADJECTIVE + AS

Form		Meaning
My mobile phone is	as expensive as yours.	the price is the same
	not as expensive as yours.	yours is more expensive

- We use *as + adjective + as* to compare two things which are the same.
  Pete's trainers are *as expensive as* mine. (they cost the same)

- We use *not as + adjective + as* to compare two things which are different.
  That dress isn't *as nice as* this one. (I prefer this one)

OTHER COMPARATIVE FORMS

Form			Meaning
Being a teenager is	a lot / far / much	harder than being a child.	a large difference
	a little / a bit / slightly		a small difference

- We use *a lot, far, slightly*, etc. to talk about how much difference there is between things which we are comparing.

QUANTIFIERS

Countable nouns	Uncountable nouns	Countable and uncountable nouns
many, (a) few, several	much, (a) little, a bit of	most (of), a lot of / lots of, plenty (of), most, any, some, more, enough, none (of), all of

- We use *much / many / few*, etc. to talk about the quantity of countable and uncountable nouns.
  I don't spend *much* time studying.
  There are *a few* good cafés in my town.

NOTE!

Some quantifiers are more often used in positive or negative sentences.

Positive sentences	Negative sentences	Positive and negative sentences
a little, a few, several, plenty of, a bit of, some, none of	much, any	most, all (of), a lot (of), enough, more, many

My friend has ~~any~~ *some* free time in the week.
I can't come out because I have ~~much~~ *a lot of* homework tonight.

Unit 4

Present Perfect Simple

Affirmative

I	've	
he / she / it	's	climbed
you / we / they	've	

Negative

I	haven't	
he / she / it	hasn't	climbed
you / we / they	haven't	

Questions

have	I	
has	he / she / it	climbed?
have	you / we / they	

We use the present perfect to talk about
- something that started in the past and continues in the present.
  I've wanted to be an explorer since I was seven.
  How long *have* you *had* a boat?
  I ~~live~~ *have lived* here since 1998.

- life experiences, when we don't say when they happened.
  We've visited South America twice.
  Have you ever *been* on a motorbike?
  I ~~never climbed~~ *have never climbed* a mountain.

- something that happened in the past that has a result in the present.
  I've left the map at home. (I haven't got the map now.)
  I ~~broke~~ *have broken* my leg, so I can't come skiing with you next week.

- We often use the present perfect with ordinal numbers (*first*, *second*, etc.) and superlatives (*biggest*, *most expensive*, etc.)
  This is the third time *I've been* bungee jumping.
  Skydiving is the most exciting thing *I've* ever *done*.

For and Since

We use *for* and *since* to talk about how long an action has continued up to the present.
- We use *for* to talk about the period of time that an action has continued.
  I've been here *for* three days / a month / a year / a long time.
  He's had a motorbike *for* two months.
  They've lived in Russia *for* ten years.

- We use *since* to talk about the moment or point in time that the action started.
  I've known how to surf *since* I was fifteen / *since* last summer / *since* I went to Cornwall.
  He's had a motorbike *since* his birthday.
  I've known my best friend *since* I was four.

Already, Just and Yet

We use *already* and *just* after *have / has* and before the past participle.
- *Already* suggests that something has happened earlier than expected; *just* means *very recently, immediately before now*.
  John has *already* finished the exam.
  She's *just* left the house.

We put *yet* at the end of the sentence. We use it with questions and negatives.
- *Yet* suggests that something hasn't happened before now, but we expect it to happen in the future.
  Have you seen the latest Harry Potter film *yet*?
  I haven't read the book *yet*.

Grammar reference 103

PRESENT PERFECT AND PAST SIMPLE

Note: for the form and use of the past simple please see page 100.

We use the present perfect to talk about
- something which started in the past and continues in the present.
  Look! I*'ve hurt* my arm! (it happened in the past, but it hurts now)

- a recent past action which has a result in the present.
  I*'ve* always *wanted* to try bungee jumping. (and that's why I'm going to try it today)

- life experiences, where we don't refer to a specific time or period.
  I*'ve* never *been* to a circus. (I haven't experienced it in my life up to now)

We use the past simple to talk about a finished action in the past.
I *enjoyed* that bungee jump that I did yesterday morning. (but I'm not still jumping now)
I often *went* to the circus as a child. (but I'm not a child now)
I *broke* my leg when I was skiing last year. (but it's not broken now)

> **NOTE!**
>
> We can use both *been* and *gone* as the past participle of the verb *to go*, but they have different meanings.
> *I've been to the supermarket.* (I went and I came back, so I have the food for tonight's dinner)
> *Dave's gone to the bank.* (he's left to go to the bank and he is still there.)

Unit 5

Note: for the form and use of the present continuous please see page 99.

WILL

Affirmative		
I / he / she / it / we / you / they	'll	learn

Negative		
I / he / she / it / we / you / they	won't	learn

Questions		
will	I / he / she / it / we / you / they	learn?

We use *will* to talk about
- decisions at the moment of speaking.
  'The window is open.'
  'I*'ll close* it.'
- general predictions.
  It*'ll rain* next week.
  You *won't like* it here.
- We can also use *shall* with the pronouns *I* and *we*, for offers and other questions.
  Shall I help you with that map? I think I know which way we should go.
  Okay, *shall* we meet up at the camp site at 3 p.m.?
  What *shall* I do about Peter? He's depending on me to help him.

GOING TO

Affirmative			
I	'm		
he / she / it	's	going to	swim
we / you / they	're		

Negative			
I	'm not		
he / she / it	isn't	going to	swim
we / you / they	aren't		

Questions			
am	I		
is	he / she / it	going to	swim?
are	we / you / they		

We use *going to* to talk about
- future intentions or plans when a decision has already been made.
  I'm *going to* get a job next year.
- predictions when there is some evidence you can see now.
  Look at the clouds. There's *going to* be a storm.

FUTURE CONTINUOUS

Affirmative			
I / he / she / it / we / you / they	will	be	listening

Negative			
I / he / she / it / we / you / they	won't	be	listening

Questions			
will	I / he / she / it / we / you / they	be	listening?

- We use the future continuous to talk about something in progress at a certain time in the future.
  'What *will* you *be doing* on Saturday evening?'
  'I*'ll be having* dinner with Sarah.'
  They*'ll be playing* football tomorrow afternoon.
- We can also use the future continuous to talk about changing trends.
  In the future, we*'ll* all *be driving* our cars even more than we do now.

FUTURE PERFECT

Affirmative			
I / he / she / it / we / you / they	will	have	understood

Negative			
I / he / she / it / we / you / they	won't	have	understood

Questions			
will	I / he / she / it / we / you / they	have	understood?

- We use the future perfect to talk about something that will be complete by a certain time in the future.
  I*'ll have finished* this letter soon.
  By the time I'm 30 I*'ll have travelled* the world.
- When we talk about future states with the future perfect, we add a time expression.
  They*'ll have had* their car for two years *next month*.
  By *next year*, I'll have ~~had~~ bought a new computer.

Grammar reference 105

Unit 6

PASSIVE: PRESENT, PAST AND PRESENT PERFECT

Active
Many people experience phobias.
Passive
Phobias are experienced by many people.

The object of an active sentence is the same as the subject of a passive sentence.

Present simple passive		
I	'm	
he / she / it	's	attacked
you / we / they	're	

Past simple passive		
I / he / she / it	was	attacked
you / we / they	were	

Present perfect simple passive			
I	've		
he / she / it	's	been	attacked
you / we / they	've		

- We form the passive with the verb *to be* + a past participle.

- We use the passive when we don't know who did the action or when we are more interested in the action.
  A new drug is being tested.
  My purse has been stolen.

- We can use *by* after a passive verb to say who or what does the action.
  It was painted by Cézanne.
  The team will be chosen by the manager.

- We use *by* + noun / gerund to talk about who does the action.
  Scientists conducted the experiment.
  The experiment was conducted by scientists.

- We don't use *by* when the person who does the action is known by everyone, or is 'people in general'.
  Helen was arrested ~~by the police~~ for shoplifting.
  Spiders and snakes are not generally liked ~~by people~~.

HAVE / GET SOMETHING DONE

Form
subject + form of *have / get* + object + past participle
Present
I'm having my hair cut tomorrow.
I don't get my flat cleaned by a cleaner. I do it myself!
Have you had your hair dyed? It looks different.
Past
Pete had his motorbike repaired last week.
Future
I won't get this room decorated this month, because I've got no spare money to pay anyone.
Are you going to get this shower fixed soon?

- We use *have / get something done* to talk about things which we ask somebody else, usually an expert or a professional, to do for us.
  I had my TV repaired because it was driving me crazy.

Unit 7

First and second conditional

First conditional
If + present simple + will + infinitive
If you see the film, you'll understand.

We use the first conditional to talk about
- possible or likely future situations.
  If it's cold tomorrow, I won't walk to college.
  If she doesn't go to the party, she won't see David.

- promises and warnings.
  If you don't go to bed now, you'll be tired tomorrow.
  If you come here at eight o'clock, I'll be ready.

Second conditional
If + past simple + would + infinitive
If you saw the film, you'd understand.

We use the second conditional
- for improbable situations now or in the future.
  If I had more money, I'd buy it for you. (It is unlikely that you will have more money.)
  If you had a car, you would learn to drive. (You don't have a car, so you won't learn to drive.)

- to give advice.
  If I were you, I'd put some suntan lotion on.
  If he lived in Germany, he'd learn German.

- In the second conditional, we can use *were* for *I*, *he*, *she*, and *it* pronouns. This use is more formal, and more common in writing than in speech.
  If he were richer, he'd be able to buy a Solo Trek.
  I would find an alternative power source if I were an inventor.

NOTE!
In all conditional sentences, the *if* clause can come before or after the main clause. The meaning is the same. If it comes before the main clause, we use a comma.
If I have time, I'll go to the exhibition.
I'll go to the exhibition if I have time.

UNLESS

- We sometimes use *unless* to join the two halves of conditional sentences. *Unless* means *if ... not*, *except if* or *only if*.
  I won't tell Maria your secret unless she asks me. (except if she asks me)
  We'll be fine unless it's raining. (if it's not raining)
  Unless we hurry, we'll miss our flight. (if we don't hurry)

- We use a present tense after *unless*, even when we are talking about the future.
  Unless they ~~will improve~~ improve the safety of this invention, it will never be a success.

Third conditional

Third conditional
If + past perfect + would have + past participle
If you had seen the film, you would have understood

- Third conditionals contain forms of *had* and *would* that are commonly abbreviated as *'d*.
  If I'd known you were at the party, I'd have talked to you. (If I had known ... I would have talked ...)

- We don't use *would* in the *if* part of the sentence.
  If I'd arrived late, I'd have missed the show. (If I ~~would have~~ had arrived late, I ~~had~~ would have missed the show)

We use the third conditional to talk about things in the past which didn't happen.
If I had known you were coming, I would have made some dinner. (I didn't know you were coming so I didn't make any dinner.)
If I hadn't bought a Playstation, I wouldn't have become so obsessed with computer games. (I bought a Playstation, and so I became obsessed with computer games)

- Using the third conditional often suggests that we regret our past actions, and like to imagine doing things differently.

Unit 8

Defining relative clauses

Relative clauses give extra information about something. The relative pronouns *who*, *which*, *that*, *where* and *whose* can introduce a relative clause.

- Defining relative clauses specify or define what is being talked about. They give extra information about someone or something.
  That's the boy who I play football with.
  The shop where I bought this top is near here.
  The computer that we bought stopped working.

- We use *who* or *that* to introduce a person. We can't use *which*.
  The man who works in the shop is very friendly.
  The girl that I met at the party had long, brown hair.
  The boy ~~which~~ *who I love works as a mechanic.*

- We use *which* or *that* to introduce a thing. We can't use *who*.
  The pen which I lost was silver.
  The car that we bought was really good.
  The book ~~who~~ *which / that I am reading at the moment is rather boring.*

- We use *whose* for possession.
  That's the woman whose son is an athlete.

- We use relative pronouns (*who*, *which*, *whose*, *where*, etc.) instead of subject / object pronouns (*he*, *she*, *it*, etc.). We can't repeat pronouns in a relative clause.
  The girl who ~~she~~ *lives next door is called Joanna.*
  That's the new CD which I bought ~~it~~ *recently.*
  There's a family in my street whose ~~their~~ *dog barks really loudly.*
  The place where I met my girlfriend ~~there~~ *is a beautiful beach.*

NOTE!

In defining relative clauses you can leave out the relative pronoun when the relative pronoun is the object of the verb.
That's the book (that) I bought. (*that* refers to *the book* and is the object of the verb *bought*)
She's the girl (who) I met. (*who* refers to *the girl* and is the object of the verb *met*)

Non-defining relative clauses

- Non-defining relative clauses give extra information which is not essential to the meaning of the sentence.
  Mr Thompson, who works in the shop, is very friendly.

- Relative pronouns must always be used in non-defining relative clauses. They can't be omitted.
  The criminal, who the police were following, escaped.

- We can join two short sentences together to make one longer sentence by using a relative pronoun.
  Alison's sister is called Debbie. She's a nurse.
  Alison's sister, who's a nurse, is called Debbie.

- We use commas to separate a non-defining relative clause from the rest of the sentence.
  We went to Bristol, where my brother used to live, at the weekend.

NOTE!

We don't use *that* in non-defining relative clauses.
My scooter, ~~that~~ *I got for my birthday last year, has never broken down.* ✗
My scooter, which I got for my birthday last year, has never broken down. ✔

Unit 9

Reported speech: statements

Direct speech	Reported speech
'I love the hotel.'	She said that she loved the hotel.
'We're having a wonderful time.'	He said that they were having a wonderful time.
'I worked for ten hours.'	He said he'd worked for ten hours.
'You've never written to me.'	She said he'd never written to her.
'I'll see you soon.'	He said he'd see her soon.

- If the reporting verb (for example *said* or *told*) is in the past, the verb in the reported statement moves back a tense into the past.
  present simple → past simple
  present continuous → past continuous
  past simple → past perfect simple
  present perfect simple → past perfect simple
  will → would
  can → could

- The modal verbs *should*, *could*, *would*, *might* and *ought to* do not change
  'We *might* come.' She said that they *might* come.
  'I *could* be there by 8.00.' He said he *could* be there by 8.00.

- Pronouns and possessive adjectives also change.
  'I'm watching *you*.' He said that he was watching *him*.
  'We've got *you* a surprise.' She said that they had got *him* a surprise.
  'I've forgotten *my* keys.' He said that he had forgotten *his* keys.

Time expressions in reported speech

Time expressions in reported speech also change.
this → that
these → those
now → then
next week → the next week
today → that day
tomorrow → the following day
yesterday → the day before
last week → the week before
before / ago → earlier
in an hour → an hour later

Reported speech: questions and commands

Direct questions	Reported questions
'What time is your train?'	She asked what the time his train was.
'Why are you laughing?'	He asked why she was laughing.

- In direct questions the word order is verb + subject.
- The word order in reported questions is subject + verb. There is no question mark.
  'How old *are you*?'
  He asked how old *she was*.
- If there is no question word in the direct question, *if* or *whether* is used in the reported question.
  'Are you Turkish?'
  He asked *if / whether* we were Turkish.

Direct commands	Reported commands
'Be quiet!'	He told them to be quiet.
'Put it out.'	She told him to put it out.

- In direct commands the imperative is used.
- In reported commands, the following form in used:
  subject + verb + object + infinitive with *to*
  She told them *to sit down*.
  He told her *to close* the window.
- To report negative commands, *not* is used before the infinitive, so the construction is:
  subject + verb + object + *not* + infinitive with *to*
  'Don't forget your wallet.'
  She told him not to forget his wallet.

Reported speech: suggestions

Direct suggestions	Reported suggestions
'Shall we go for a walk?'	He suggested that they went for a walk.
'Why don't we go out tonight?'	She suggested going out that night.

We use the reporting verb *suggest* in reported suggestions.

Grammar reference 109

Unit 10

Modal: Ability

Modal	Example	Use
can	I can speak French.	To talk about ability in the present.
will be able to	I won't be able to play football because I've hurt my leg.	To talk about ability in the future.
could	Matt could talk when he was three.	To talk about ability in the past.

- *Be able to* has infinitive, gerund and past participle forms, so it can be used with perfect tenses, and in constructions where it is impossible to use *can*.
  I've always ~~can~~ been able to swim.
  ~~Can~~ Being able to drive is essential if you want this job.
  I'd like to ~~can~~ be able to speak three or four languages.

- *Could* is used for general ability in the past, but can't be used for ability on specific occasions. We use *managed to* or *was able to*.
  I was exhausted and very cold, but at last I ~~could~~ was able to / managed to reach the top of the mountain.

Modals: Obligation, Advice and Prohibition

Modal	Example	Use
must / have to	You must remember your homework. / I have to finish this essay by Monday.	To talk about an obligation.
don't have to	You don't have to come if you don't want to.	To say that there is no obligation to do something.
ought to / should / shouldn't	You ought to wear red. You should think about going on holiday. You shouldn't worry so much.	To give advice.
mustn't	You mustn't smoke in here.	To talk about prohibition.

> **NOTE!**
> *have to* and *must* have similar meaning but *don't have to* and *mustn't* have different meanings.

You *mustn't* touch the paintings at the gallery. (there is an obligation not to do this)
You *don't have to* come to the park if you don't want to. (there is no obligation, so you can choose what you would prefer to do)

Modals: Possibility and Certainty

Modal	Example	Use
may / might / could	You may be right. He might already know. They could be on the train.	To say something is possible in the present or future.
can't	It can't be finished.	To say something is impossible.
must	You must be her daughter.	To say we are sure something is true.

- We only use the negative form *can't* when we are talking about possibility. We can't use *can* to say that something is possible.
  He ~~can~~ could be at the bus station by now.

- We only use the positive form *must* when we are talking about possibility. We can't use *mustn't* to say that something is impossible.
  Katie ~~mustn't~~ can't be in, because she's not answering the phone.

- *Could* and *might* / *may* have very similar meanings.
  Paul *could be* / *might be* / *may be* at home.

Modals + Perfect Infinitive

Modal	Example	Use
may have / might have / could have	She may have forgotten. We might have caught the plane. We could have crashed.	To say something was possible in the past.
can't have	She can't have missed the bus. She left early.	To say something was impossible in the past.
must have	It's here. He must have left it behind.	To say that we are sure something was true in the past

Irregular verbs

Infinitive	Past tense	Past participle
be	was / were	been
become	became	become
begin	began	begun
break	broke	broken
bring	brought	brought
build	built	built
buy	bought	bought
can	could	could
catch	caught	caught
come	came	come
cost	cost	cost
cut	cut	cut
do	did	done
dream	dreamt / dreamed	dreamt / dreamed
drive	drove	driven
eat	ate	eaten
fall	fell	fallen
feed	fed	fed
feel	felt	felt
fight	fought	fought
find	found	found
fly	flew	flown
forget	forgot	forgotten
get	got	got
give	gave	given
go	went	gone
have	had	had
hear	heard	heard
hide	hid	hidden
hit	hit	hit
hold	held	held
hurt	hurt	hurt
keep	kept	kept
know	knew	known
learn	learnt / learned	learnt / learned
leave	left	left
lend	lent	lent
let	let	let
lie	lay	lain
lose	lost	lost
make	made	made
mean	meant	meant
meet	met	met
pay	paid	paid
put	put	put
read	read	read
ring	rang	rung
ride	rode	ridden
run	ran	run
say	said	said

Infinitive	Past tense	Past participle
see	saw	seen
sell	sold	sold
send	sent	sent
set	set	set
shake	shook	shaken
shine	shone	shone
show	showed	shown / showed
shut	shut	shut
sing	sang	sung
sit	sat	sat
sleep	slept	slept
speak	spoke	spoken
spend	spent	spent
split	split	split
spread	spread	spread
stand	stood	stood
steal	stole	stolen
swim	swam	swum
take	took	taken
teach	taught	taught
tell	told	told
think	thought	thought
throw	threw	thrown
try	tried	tried
understand	understood	understood
wear	wore	worn
win	won	won
write	wrote	written

OXFORD
UNIVERSITY PRESS

Great Clarendon Street, Oxford OX2 6DP

Oxford University Press is a department of the University of Oxford.
It furthers the University's objective of excellence in research, scholarship,
and education by publishing worldwide in

Oxford New York

Auckland Cape Town Dar es Salaam Hong Kong Karachi
Kuala Lumpur Madrid Melbourne Mexico City Nairobi
New Delhi Shanghai Taipei Toronto

With offices in

Argentina Austria Brazil Chile Czech Republic France Greece
Guatemala Hungary Italy Japan Poland Portugal Singapore
South Korea Switzerland Thailand Turkey Ukraine Vietnam

OXFORD and OXFORD ENGLISH are registered trade marks of
Oxford University Press in the UK and in certain other countries

© Oxford University Press 2003

The moral rights of the author have been asserted

Database right Oxford University Press (maker)

First published 2003

2009 2008 2007 2006 2005

10 9 8 7 6 5 4 3 2

All rights reserved. No part of this publication may be reproduced, stored in a retrieval system, or transmitted, in any form or by any means, without the prior permission in writing of Oxford University Press (with the sole exception of photocopying carried out under the conditions stated in the paragraph headed 'Photocopying'), or as expressly permitted by law, or under terms agreed with the appropriate reprographics rights organization. Enquiries concerning reproduction outside the scope of the above should be sent to the ELT Rights Department, Oxford University Press, at the address above

You must not circulate this book in any other binding or cover and you must impose this same condition on any acquirer

Photocopying

The Publisher grants permission for the photocopying of those pages marked 'photocopiable' according to the following conditions. Individual purchasers may make copies for their own use or for use by classes that they teach. School purchasers may make copies for use by staff and students, but this permission does not extend to additional schools or branches

Under no circumstances may any part of this book be photocopied for resale

Any websites referred to in this publication are in the public domain and their addresses are provided by Oxford University Press for information only. Oxford University Press disclaims any responsibility for the content

ISBN-13: 978 0 19 431050 5
ISBN-10: 0 19 431050 7

Printed in Spain by Just Colour Graphic, S. L.

ACKNOWLEDGEMENTS

Illustrations by: Clinton Banbury pp. 9, 10, 27 (biker), 32, 35, 61 (inventor), 68 (washing), 80, 82, 87, 89 (music); Will Barras pp. 14 (boy), 18, 42, 54 (boy), 68 (girls), 69, 78, 86; Mark Duffin pp. 7, 24, 64, 65, 73; Simon Gurr pp. 17, 26, 27 (girl), 28, 33, 61 (class), 83; Hardlines p. 75; Nick Hawken pp. 44, 46; Tim Kahane pp. 43, 60; Richard Lyon p. 53; Joel Morris pp. 15, 51, 79 (boy), 81; Mike Roberts pp. 14 (girl), 36, 72, 89; Jonathan Williams pp. 29, 54 (car), 79 (car).

Location Photography: Rob Judges p. 5.

The publishers would like to thank the following for their kind permission to reproduce photographs and other copyright material: Advertising Archives p. 63 (Kodak Eastman); Alamy pp. 40 (forest fire/A. T. Willett), 76 (ferry/Ali Kabas, tram/ Christine Osborne), 78 (backpacker/R. Llewellyn); Ardea pp. 8 (cockroaches), 48 (pigeons, rattlesnake), 49 (spider), 50 (tarantula, shark); Aviation Images p.16 (pilot's licence cover/Mark Wagner); BIG Pictures pp. 96 (Tina Cousins), 97 (Avril Lavigne), 98 ('N sync); Corbis pp. 4 (dog/Don Mason), 16 (light aircraft/James A Sugar), 20 (Eurostar/Owen Franken), 37 (amusement park/Jan Butchofsky-Houser), 42 (fire warning/Jay Syverson), 58 (refrigerators/Schenectady Museum; Hall of Electrical History Foundation), 66 (rastafarian/Bob Krist); Corbis Stock Market p. 86 (chimp/Dennis Blachut); Eye Ubiquitous p. 51 (Malaysia), 77 (street scene); FoodPix p. 4 (Baklava/Brian Leatart); Image100 p. 63 (boy playing video game); Impact Photos p.13 (newspaper boy); Mary Evans Picture Library p. 58 (monk copying manuscript); Masterfile p. 92 (man/Ron Fehling); National Geographic p. 57 (lightning/Joel Sartore); Oxford Scientific Films pp.40 (earthquake, floods), 41 (fire fighter); Photodisc pp. 4 (newspaper stand), 12 (architect), 13 (waitress), 23 (teens shopping), 51 (young woman), 62 (computer store), 71 (tattooed woman); Pictor International pp. 4 (family eating outside/ Paddy Eckersley), 9 (female portrait, Trinity College/Ethel Davies), 10 (Canada), 18 (woman interviewer/Paddy Eckersley), 33 (snowboarder/John Kelly, windsurfer, bungee jumper, sky diving/Jerry Irwin, hang gliding), 48 (lightning), 77 (Sydney, kangaroo sign/Photographer 37, service station); Popperfoto pp. 31 (Davo Karnicar, Jim Shekhdar), 34 (Tino Wallenda), 41 (firefighters), 76 (Spanish pop star); PYMCA pp. 66 (punks/ Derek Ridgers), 70 (boots/Derek Ridgers); Redferns pp. 94 (Otis Redding/ Michael Ochs Archives), 95 (Britney Spears/Bob King); Rex Features pp. 12 (postman), 66 (hippy, skinhead), 70 (Milan fashion show, postman), 85 (Big Brother 3); Science Photo Library pp. 12 (nurse/ BSIP, Laurent), 40 (drought/ Dr Jeremy Burgess), 44 (volcanic crater/ Bernhard Edmaier), 45 (volcanologist), 47 (map of Earth/Tony Craddock), 52 (Apollo 13/NASA), 58 (first flight/US Library of Congress); Science & Society Picture Library p. 58 (Sony Walkman, Walker's Friction Lights, mobile phone/Science Museum); Stone pp. 5 (young woman/John Lamb), 6 (Eilan Donan Castle/Duncan McNicol), 8 (teenage boy/Chris Bale), 12 (greengrocer/Adrian Weinbrecht, mechanic/Christopher Bissell), 22 (school class/David Young-Wolff), 23 (twins playing computer game/Betsie Van der Meer), 25 (boy studying/Kevin Morris), 33 (abseiling/Phil Schermeister), 43 (paper mill/Larry Goldstein), 66 (biker/Andy Sacks), 67 (teenage girls/Philip Lee Harvey), 69 (girl with pink hair/Lelande Bobbe); Taxi pp. 13 (window cleaner/Michael Malyszko), 21 (hairdresser/Peter Beavis), 23 (night club/ Willie Maldonado, two teens/V. C. L.), 25 (classroom/Tony Anderson), 30 (diving with shark/David Fleetham, hang glider/David Fleetham, climber/ Anne-Marie Weber), 39 (student/Dick Makin), 65 (scientist/Ffoto Fictions), 67 (skateboarders/Ron Chapple); The Image Bank pp. 8 (Tibetan monk/ D.E.Cox), 11 (girl bodyboarding/Matthias Clamer), 12 (engineer inside engine/V.C.L., hairdresser/ Andy Bullock), 16 (teenage boy/Dennis Galante), 22 (teenagers cycling/Peter Cade), 23 (girl with mobile phone/Steve Dunwell), 30 (sailor/Jeff Sherman), 35 (knife thrower's assistant), 40 (water pollution/Guido Alberto Rossi), 41 (helicopter over forest/Marc Solomon), 48 (man on top of high building/Alan Thornton, people in elevator/Andrew Yates Productions), 49 (man wearing white vest/James Day), 68 (micro-scooter/Romilly Lockyer), 76 (helicopter/ Weinberg, coach/A&L Sinibaldi, scooter/Craig Cameron Olsen), 84 (crowd of fans/ Robert Daly, chauffeur/ Philip Lee Harvey), 85 (man in suit/Robert Daly, paparazzi/ Michael Krasowitz), 90 (teens singing/Christopher Wilhelm); The Ronald Grant Archive pp. 48 (Blair Witch Project poster), 52 (Apollo 13 poster), 59 (Thunderball/Eon Productions).

Special thanks to: Carlo Little p.88; Warren Wettenstein p. 59

The authors and publisher are grateful to those who have given permission to reproduce the following extracts and adaptations of copyright material: p. 95 I'm Not A Girl, Not Yet A Woman. Words and Music by Dido Armstrong, Max Martin and Rami Jacoub © 2001 Maratone / Zomba Music Publishers Ltd, London (70%) and Warner/Chappell Music Ltd, London W6 8BS (30%) Reproduced by permission of Music Sales Ltd and International Music Publications Ltd All Rights Reserved. International Copyright Secured.

p. 96 Nothing to Fear. by Tina Cousins. © All Boys Music Ltd, London. Reproduced by permission.

p. 97 Sk8er Boi. Words and Music by Lauren Christy, David Alspach, Graham Edwards and Avril Lavigne © 2002 Rainbow Fish Music, Ferry Hill Songs, Mr Spock Music and Almo-Music Corp, USA (75%) Warner/Chappell North America Ltd, London W6 8BS. Rondor Music (London) Ltd, (25%). Reproduced by permission of International Music Publications Ltd and Music Sales Ltd. All Rights Reserved. International Copyright Secured.

p. 98 Celebrity. Words and Music by Wade Robson, Jimmy Newt and Justin Timberlake © 2001 Wajero Sound, Valentine's Day Songs, Tennman Tunes and Zomba Songs Inc, USA (33.34%) Warner/Chappell Artemis Music Ltd, London W6 8BS (33.33%) Warner/Chappell North America Ltd, London W6 8BS. Zomba Music Ltd, London (33.3%). Reproduced by permission of International Music Publications Ltd and Music Sales Ltd. All Rights Reserved. International Copyright Secured.

p. 94 (Sittin' On) The Dock Of The Bay. Words and Music by Otis Redding and Steve Cropper © 1967 / 1968 Cotillion Music Corp, East Memphis Music Corp and Irving Music Inc, USA, Rondor Music (London) Ltd (75%), Warner/Chappell Music Ltd, London W6 8BS (25%). Reproduced by permission of Music Sales Ltd and International Music Publications Ltd All Rights Reserved. International Copyright Secured.

p. 31 'Climber to ski down Everest' by Oliver August © Times Newspapers Ltd, London 6 October 2000. Reproduced by permission.

p. 31 'Briton fights sharks in Pacific rowing marathon' by Diana Taylor, © Reuters Ltd 30 March 2001. Reproduced by permission. All rights reserved.

p. 34 Information about The Flying Wallendas from www.wallenda.com. Reproduced by permission of Tino Wallenda.

p. 59 Information about SoloTrek XFV' from www.solotrek.com. Reproduced by permission of Trek Aerospace.

p. 88 'Drummer who said no to The Stones' by Russell Newmark, © The Independent 22 March 2003. Reproduced by permission.

Although every effort has been made to trace and contact copyright holders before publication, this has not been possible in some cases. We apologize for any apparent infringement of copyright and if notified, the publisher will be pleased to rectify any errors or omissions at the earliest opportunity.